REMEMBERING THE FUTURE

IMAGINING THE PAST

REMEMBERING THE FUTURE
IMAGINING THE PAST

Story, Ritual, and the Human Brain

DAVID A. HOGUE

WIPF & STOCK · Eugene, Oregon

Wipf and Stock Publishers
199 W 8th Ave, Suite 3
Eugene, OR 97401

Remembering the Future, Imagining the Past
Story, Ritual, and the Human Brain
By Hogue, David A.
Copyright©2003 Pilgrim Press
ISBN 13: 978-1-60608-860-9
Publication date 6/10/2009
Previously published by Pilgrim Press, 2003

Contents

Acknowledgments

My interest in the sciences has been lifelong, and my particular interest in the neurosciences and ritual studies first developed during graduate school. The current volume had its start in 2000 as the Roland S. Boreham Jr. Lectures in Pastoral Care at the Sparks Health System, Ft. Smith, Arkansas, at the invitation of Chaplain Don Hubbard. The positive response to this material prompted my continued interest and thinking. In addition, portions of this material were presented at Garrett-Evangelical Theological Seminary; Columbia Theological Seminary; the Krist Samaritan Counseling Center of Clear Lake, Texas, at the invitation of Executive Director Gerald DeSobe; the Person, Culture and Religion Working Group of the American Academy of Religion; and the Society for Pastoral Theology. The questions, critiques, and support from participants in each of these settings have contributed immeasurably to both the form and content of this work.

Two men in particular have been models for their personal and professional investments in the brain sciences and their relevance to making sense of human experience. Eliezer Schwartz, of the then Illinois School of Professional Psychology, Chicago, first introduced me to the content and clinical relevance of neuropsychology during my postdoctoral work. He later became a colleague as well as an instructor. The late James Ashbrook, a colleague at Garrett-Evangelical Theological Seminary, Evanston, Illinois, was a pioneer in relating the emerging brain sciences to the practices of pastoral care and counseling and indeed to the enterprise of constructive theology. I am indebted to both men.

It is a cliché to note that any work of this sort would not have been possible without the help of colleagues, friends, and family. Nonetheless, clichés often survive because of the truths they express. Neal Fisher, president; Jack Seymour, dean; and the board of trustees of Garrett-Evangelical Theological Seminary provided two sabbaticals for the development of this work. Colleagues Dwight and Linda Vogel share with me their lifelong interests in worship and ritual studies. Publisher Timothy Staveteig of Pilgrim Press has listened for several years to my dreams for this volume, and editor Ulrike Guthrie has graciously helped see it to completion. George Graham, then of Pilgrim Press, encouraged the development of this project. Friends Arlis McLean and Michael Melton graciously offered their home in Tucson, Arizona, for a spring of uninterrupted writing. Labar Farber was graciously helpful in preparation of some of the figures for this volume, and Ann Rosewall assisted with the index. I am deeply grateful to colleagues who have read all or parts of drafts, including Cliff Guthrie, Christie Neuger, Lem Rees, and Dwight Judy. Their comments and encouragements have made my work stronger, though I must of course bear the responsibility for its content and accuracy.

It is an understatement to say that this book would never have seen the light of day were it not for my wife, Diane Stephens. Her questions about the implications of memory, imagination, and storytelling for spiritual practices helped focus my writing, and her knowledge of spiritual formation particularly enriched chapter 6. She encouraged my interests, read and commented on multiple drafts, and most important, as a writer, understood the emotional ups and downs of writing. Hopefully this volume will give voice to my gratitude.

Introduction

In 1995 eight-year-old Christina Santhouse lost the right half of her brain. She suffered from a rare disease known as Rasmussen's encephalitis which would have eventually left her "very debilitated, very handicapped and quite retarded," according to Dr. John Freeman, one of her physicians. She was already having more than one hundred seizures per day. After trying antiseizure medication for several months to no avail, Christina and her mother finally chose the radical step of a hemispherectomy, a procedure in which the right half of her brain was removed in a fourteen-hour operation. Today, she is seizure-free and an A student in high school; Christina also bowls on the varsity team.[1]

The marvels of the human brain have filled the pages of newspapers and the Internet, television screens and radio waves with reports on more than a decade of explosive research into the workings of the three pounds of gray and white matter that is responsible for our thinking, feeling, and planning, indeed for much of what makes us human. We've gazed at colorful computer-drawn illustrations of brains on drugs, brains doing meditation, and brains concentrating on an intensive task. We've witnessed the development of new medications that target neurotransmitters to relieve depression, Parkinson's disease, and schizophrenia. We've heard promises of even more startling treatments for Alzheimer's disease and epilepsy. We've read descriptions and speculations about the way the two hemispheres of our brains work differently and wondered whether we might even have two brains. Christina's story makes it all personal.

---

1. Michael Rubinkam, Associated Press, October 7, 2001.

"I've had some weak moments, when I feel sorry for myself and think I have the worst luck, but this happened for a reason."

Though Christina's outcomes are far from perfect (she has left-side paralysis, loss of peripheral vision on her left side — and after rapid head movements she hears the "whoosh" of the spinal fluid with which doctors replaced the missing brain tissue), the very fact that she is able to function at all, let alone as well as she does, is remarkable. That a brain can survive such trauma is reassuring. That it can restructure itself to perform the critical functions of mental life and memory is miraculous.

Neuroscientists are still in the early stages of discovering what the brain can do and how it operates. Exciting technologies like magnetic resonance imaging (MRI) and positron emission tomography (PET scans) have enabled scientists to peer inside the brains of living, thinking human beings rather than waiting for the opportunity to perform autopsies. Daily we are learning about the role different areas of our brain play in making decisions, in recognizing the faces of those we love, and even in experiencing God. What transformative new insights might such discoveries offer to our understandings of worship and pastoral care?

The future of such research is at once exhilarating and frightening, even confusing at times. While the language used to describe the brain is often esoteric and frequently overwhelming, the ongoing discoveries that language describes hold immense hope for those who pray for relief from a variety of mental and physical illnesses. Such research holds untold promise for better ways to teach our children, organize our work settings, and relate to each other. We are led to believe that someday we may even be able to "customize" our own personalities through biomedical interventions. At the same time, we fear being reduced to computer-like machines that can only be serviced by neuroscience technicians, or having our minds read by X-ray machines. We wonder whether in the future it will do any good to talk about our problems; perhaps what we will really need is a pill to solve them for us automatically.

Human Nature

Almost every day, these discoveries about the human brain are forcing us to rethink our understandings of the meaning and uniqueness of human experience. In the study of our brains, we are confronted by the ways we are similar to other animals, yet know that we are different. The age-old question, "What is humanity that God is mindful of us?" comes to mind for those of us steeped in the language of the Psalms. Just as the first landing of the Apollo 11 astronauts on the moon in 1969 reshaped forever how we understand ourselves and our place in the universe, so the explosion of new findings about the brain is pressing us for new and deeper understandings of who we are and what it means to be human.

The neurosciences are making remarkable contributions to our dynamic understandings of human nature — that is, to our developing theological anthropologies. The debate is a serious one. As neuroscientific discoveries describe with increasing precision the structures and activities of our complex human brains during religious experiences like meditation, prayer, and moral reasoning, many will interpret these findings as reducing life's profoundest experiences to the more or less organized firing of neurons. Because we can understand the neurological basis of religious experience, some will argue that positing any transcendent reality outside of our brains is extraneous; we no longer have any need for God. For these persons, science will have pushed back the cloud of mystery from phenomena that religious dogma used to explain.

Others will argue just as persuasively that the sciences are once again merely "tracing God's fingertips," uncovering the consequences in the brain of divine activity. For these people, science serves as a confirmation of faith. Yet we can no longer afford to ignore science's discoveries about the brain any more than we can afford to ignore the discoveries of astronomy and physics. Without conversation with the sciences in general, and the life sciences in particular, we have an incomplete picture of who we are.

The sheer volume of information about the brain, its functions, its capacities, and its vulnerabilities is overwhelming. This book, therefore, focuses on two key areas of discovery and their implications for religious life and practice: memory and imagination. We are our memories; the events of life that we recall give us a sense of personal identity and movement through time. For better and for worse, we are shaped and transformed by our experiences through the synaptic patterns with which our brains record those experiences. As we recall the stories that have brought us to any given moment in time, we are both rediscovering and proclaiming who we are.

But life and identity are not limited to the events of history; we constantly live on the cusp between the past and the future. The human brain is endowed with the unique capacity to construct images of what could be as well as perceptions of what is. We are not chained to the present and the presently "real"; we can also imagine the unreal and the "not-yet-real." So imagination is the grounding of hope. Without the capacity to envision life in ways that are different from the ways it is now, we are tethered to the struggles of the present. Imagination provides visions of redemption and release. But imagination is also the grounding of fear and despair; we can envision not only a more promising future but a more terrifying or hopeless one. At their best, such imaginings can help us to avoid danger or to prepare for the suffering that is inevitable in life; they can also rob life of the joy that would otherwise be available for abundant living.

Memory and imagination are not separate processes. Rather, they are linked in a vital, dynamic way. Our imaginations are as essential when we are recalling the past as when we are speculating about or planning for the future. And without memories, our dreams for what may yet be would be empty and impossible. We imagine the past and we remember the future. Christian theology has spoken of the sacred uniqueness of individuals through the notion of the soul. The brain sciences are underscoring for us a truth we have known all along: our souls exist at the intersection of our memories and our imaginations, on the ever-moving point between the past and the present.

Memory and imagination are not the sole province of individuals. Remembered stories also shape our families, our communities of faith, and our national identities. Our larger communities have dreams and visions of what is and of what is yet to come. We tell our stories to each other and teach them to our children. We hold steadfastly to our images of what could or even should be right now; we live out our visions of what could be in the time to come.

Failures of memory and imagination are at the heart of much human suffering. Some remembered experiences threaten our sense of grace or of trust. Lost or missing memories undermine our sense of completeness or uniqueness. Some imagined scenarios inspire acceptance and appreciation, while others lead to guilt and shame. Some envisioned scenes foster hope and growth, while others lead to despair and resignation. Lack of ability to imagine alternatives is frequently a central characteristic of people who suffer depression and who consider suicide.

Memory and imagination both have deep roots within the Christian tradition as well as in most of the world's major religions. The word "remember" appears at least two hundred times in the New Revised Standard Version of the Bible. The word "imagination" appears only four times, and in each case it is associated with evil or idolatry! The word "vision," on the other hand, fits more closely with our modern-day use of the word "imagination" and neatly includes the experience of dreams as well as images of truths not available through the five senses. "Vision" appears eighty-seven times.

While human beings may not be the only species capable of these interlocking capacities, we are able to utilize them more than any other species does. We remember more, we communicate more through language, and we can imagine a much wider range of scenarios than the great ape or the bonobo monkey. What then are the implications of memory and imagination for religious experience? And what do they teach us that can inform us about the ways we care for each other, how we worship together, and how we connect to the transcendent experiences that are signatures of being human? These are some of the questions at the heart of this volume.

So in the pages that follow, we explore current understandings of perceiving, remembering, and imagining — the three primary ways we human beings make sense of ourselves and the world in which we must live. The human brain by its very nature must make meaning of the world and of the "owner's" place in that world. We consider the difficulties our brains encounter in distinguishing "fact from fiction" and the dangers those difficulties entail. But we also look to the promising possibilities that flow from such a dilemma — the ways our imaginations can also draw us into an as-yet-unrealized future. Indeed, imagination is a necessary capacity in language and all symbolic communication, including religious experience, story, and ritual. Imagination goes beyond anticipating future stories to include the constructs we build of the past and present. Our imaginative brains draw maps of the world around us that give us direction, and, for the most part, those maps bear a striking resemblance to the territories they describe. Yet because maps are pictures of the land and not the land itself, our brains constantly sketch and revise them, tracing old routes and charting new paths.

The Context

This work has grown out of my long-standing interest in the roles of the neurosciences and ritual studies because of their implications for the practices of the church. How do our brains envision unseen realities like God, peace, or forgiveness and help us live into them? While taking an introductory course in neuropsychology, I first encountered possibilities to appreciate the embodied nature of human experience and of religious experience in particular. The brain sciences turned on lights, illuminating new facets of the pastoral counseling endeavor, of worship, and of humanness itself. While our religious traditions have their distinctive histories and sacred texts and we often identify ourselves based on those differences, there are also shared dimensions to experiences of the divine. Neuroscientific discoveries regarding the brain's perception, memory, and imagination, like studies in the psychology of religion, point to experiences common to all human beings.

As a pastoral theologian and counselor, I have come to value the significant resources of the brain sciences for the work of the church in guiding, healing, and challenging persons and systems, resources that are informed by our current understandings of the central nervous system. So I read this material from the perspective of one whose primary concern is the sustaining, healing, guiding, and reconciling of human beings within the context of transcendent meaning and purpose. Given that pastoral caregivers have incorporated the best of the sciences of their day throughout the church's history,[2] our tradition invites us to inquire about important new discoveries as we reflect critically on the practices of the church. In what ways do the neurosciences and ritual studies inform religious practice and leadership? What can we learn further about the ways the body and the brain take part in and shape ritual and liturgy? What do the brain sciences have to say to our practices of care and counseling? What are the practical implications of unfolding neuroscientific discoveries for religious life?

Evolution and the Brain

Most neuroscientific exploration assumes the foundation of evolutionary theory for the questions scientists ask and the ways they go about answering those questions. Evolutionary theory has mapped the progressive adaptation of life over millions of years, leading from single-cell plants to human life as we now know it. An underlying assumption of evolutionary theory is that changes in an organism that

---

2. William A. Clebsch and Charles R. Jaekle, *Pastoral Care in Historical Perspective* (New York: Harper Torchbooks, 1967), 4.

increase its likelihood of survival will be passed on to subsequent generations, resulting in increasingly complex and adaptive organisms. Structures and functions of the human brain are described with attention to how they might have contributed survival advantages to the human species.

Religious and scientific thinkers have historically been on opposite sides in debates over the validity of evolutionary theory. In recent decades, a significant number of theologians and scientists have engaged in productive dialogue to the enhancement of the work of both disciplines. This volume assumes the validity of that dialogue.

At the same time, one can appreciate the contributions of the brain sciences without an uncritical acceptance of the evolutionary assumptions behind them. Science is never value-neutral. Nevertheless, the discoveries of the role of the brain in shaping our experience can be absorbed despite their theoretical grounding in evolutionary biology. Most if not all of the recent discoveries about the brain can support the celebration of a created universe as well as an evolving one.

The Risks of Speculation

One dilemma confronting anyone who would learn from the neurosciences (and hope to make specific applications to any dimension of life experience) is the temptation to make claims well beyond what the science will support. No clearer example of such speculation can be cited than the responses to Roger Sperry's split-brain research in the 1960s and 1970s. Right-brain and left-brain distinctions became a centerpiece on the cultural landscape, and some writers found application to nearly every experience of humankind, including personality. Untested claims and techniques, supposedly inspired by this landmark research, became the order of the day.

We could avoid that risk by refusing to make any claims at all about the implications of these fascinating discoveries. But we would pay for our safety with an accumulation of interesting facts about the brain which would make little or no difference in life. Too severe a caution about speculation can lead to saying nothing at all. If we choose to wait for the maturity of the sciences so that we can make applications with nearly absolute confidence, we will never get there. And it is often in the attempted applications of science that their conclusions are most adequately tested. Finally, applications of the findings of science are a way for practitioners to ask their own questions of research, rather than to stand by, hoping that science will ask the right questions. So my intent in this volume is to remain as close to the science as possible while pondering the potential ways these findings may make specific contributions to the practices of faith.

The Task at Hand

Imagination, memory, and story interact in unique and transformative ways in the ritual experiences of life. The historic practices of pastoral counseling, worship, and the spiritual disciplines, mediated through the brain, are enriched when we reclaim the effective power of ritual for individuals and for communities of faith. In the pages ahead, we explore each dimension of ritual experience and finally attempt to draw out new images of the spiritual practices of soul tending, informed by contemporary science. The task is an exciting, if daunting, one.

The first three chapters of this volume lay important groundwork for understanding our experiences of rituals of transformation. Chapter 1 briefly introduces the categories of perception, memory, and imagination. The centerpiece of the chapter is an exploration of the marvels of our unique human capacity to construct images of possibilities far removed from present realities.

Chapter 2 tends to matters of memory, including its strengths and its vulnerabilities. Because memories are so critical to our identities as persons and as communities, we explore the tasks that human memory performs well and those with which memory struggles. Memories are central to the practices of care and counseling in which the church engages daily. Central to this chapter is the conviction that memories are reconstructed every time they are recalled. We also explore ways memory and imagination intersect to create our experiences of soul.

In chapter 3, we enter the realm of stories which embody our memories and our imaginations. Our brains are inveterate story-tellers. Stories structure our experiences of selfhood and provide opportunities for change in the acts of telling, listening to, and reflecting on our stories. Narrative pastoral theology is a central method for comprehending the ways stories shape who we are as persons and as communities. Like memories, stories are reconstructed as they are told. The dynamic nature of stories introduces methods for transformation and hope in our self-understanding.

The structure and power of rituals form the central message of chapter 4. Just as our brains are constantly telling stories, so too are they natural ritualizers. Story and action are joined together in ritual, embodying the stories and memories of our communities and of personal experience. Planting a flower following a miscarriage tells an all-too-brief story, much like the eucharist embodies the story of Christ's presence among communities of faith. Since our brains innately ritualize life experiences, we discover that rituals provide a time and place where the norms of everyday living are temporarily suspended — a liminal space. Under these unique circumstances we temporarily enter a world remarkably different from the one we regularly inhabit. Though our time in liminal space comes to an end, we return to the routine as changed persons. Pastoral counseling, spiritual practice, and worship all partake of these qualities of ritual.

Chapters 5 and 6 draw together the implications of earlier chapters and step out onto a limb of cautious speculation. What do the findings of ritual studies and the neurosciences suggest about the ways we practice faith? As we continue to learn about what makes our brains tick, how can we enrich our experiences of worship, care, direction, and spiritual discipline?

Viewing religious practice through the lens of the brain can seem a dangerous task. We risk reducing our comprehensions of faith to the interactions of chemicals and neurons and tissue. Further, we risk substituting the methods of theology with the methods and values of science. Such dialogue must always be a two-way conversation; theology and the church must be asking critical questions of the sciences as well. Communities of faith must always test the newest discoveries against the wisdom of the centuries. But entering deeply into an exploration of the inner world of the brain promises experiences of awe and reverence for the embodied activity of God unavailable in any other way. As the late James Ashbrook declared, "What we are learning about the human brain makes more understandable the longings of the human heart."[3]

---

3. James Ashbrook, *Minding the Soul: Pastoral Counseling as Remembering* (Minneapolis: Fortress Press, 1996), xviii.

Chapter 1

WHAT IF...?
Imagination and the Brain

We live in the world of the imagination as fully, as spiritedly, as much with the organs of the body as we do in the blood and sinew activities of daily life. —Ann and Barry Ulanov[1]

Observing. Remembering. Imagining. Daily living depends on these three processes of mind, and we pride ourselves on being able to make clear distinctions between them. For the most part we make those distinctions with confidence. There is, at least in our day-to-day believing and living, a wide gulf fixed between the three processes. Present. Past. Future.

We see what is happening in front of us right now. From my office window I see bright sunshine washing over the deep green leaves that swing gently in the wind outside. Most of the time we trust what we are observing, because seeing is believing. What we remember on the other hand has already occurred. Those events, people, places, and pictures are locked forever in the archives of our brains — some with brilliant unfaded colors, some gathering dust, some getting a little clouded over with the passage of time, but in there nonetheless. When we need those memories, we expect to be able to go back to the files in our brains and pull them out.

Our imaginations are another thing altogether — at least as we normally think of imagination. Imagination is less concerned with

1. Ann and Barry Ulanov, *The Healing Imagination: The Meeting of Psyche and Soul* (Einsiedeln, Switzerland: Daimon, 1999), 148.

what is, or has been, than with what could be. It is less concerned with established facts and more with possibility. That bright sun and gentle breeze outside my window evoke images of a summer run or a warming nap in the backyard. Or I might imagine gentle spirits stroking the nearby trees, or God smiling on creation. Accuracy and precision are no longer imagination's primary concerns; creativity and playfulness are its characteristic marks. Memory focuses on logical consistency; imagination calls on the absurd or at least the nonrational. Stories or events or relationships that are impossible in the real world *can work* — and even make sense — in the wonderful world of the imagination.

Perception lets us know what's out there — what's going on in the world that is important to our survival, to our well-being. Memory maps our world and tells us where the treasures and dangers are. Imagination is the stage on which we play out what could be, the field of spontaneous play where the limitations of the real world are suspended for a time. In imagination, we make our way to relief and escape — or sometimes to scenes of anxiety or terror. Bright sunshine might also evoke images of burning or a dangerous cancer growing in unprotected skin. Memory relates to the experienced past; imagination relates to the future, and sometimes to the past we might have experienced. Memory and imagination have become polar opposites for us in our daily experience.

The accuracy of memory is highly favored in North America over the constructions of the imagination. "Just the facts, Ma'am," is more than a frequent comment of Sergeant Joe Friday on *Dragnet;* it is the mantra of a post-Enlightenment society. We declare to ourselves or to others, "That's just a figment of your imagination," or we say to a hypochondriacal friend, "You're not really sick. It's all in your head." Much of our mental life is spent trying to separate fact from fiction, getting to the truth, or being in touch with what is "real" rather than that which is "imaginary." We decry and prosecute the creative accounting of accountants, financial consultants, and chief executive officers who create false impressions of the health of organizations.

Or we conclude that imagination is the sole province of children or of gifted artists and poets. Some people have it, and others don't. The world of the imaginary is a paradise from which we were driven as we moved into the world of adulthood, where bills must be paid, responsibilities fulfilled, and where living is by the sweat of our brows. We contain the power of the imagination by valuing it in those who by choice or by compulsion give expression to creative power in ways that tap our own desire for the imaginary — and our own ambivalence about it. We go to concerts and plays, readings and galleries, pleased that some among us can help fulfill the creative needs of our communities — while the rest of us do real work and pay the bills.

Imagination is not merely a source of pleasure. The creations of our minds can frighten as well as inspire and comfort us. Anxiety is frequently one of the consequences of the imagination, grounded in the fearful events that our minds conjure, even when we cannot identify exactly what catastrophe the mind is anticipating. We both envy and fear the imagination; we can be literally enchanted by the creations of the mind and soul and terrified by them as well.

The uneven valuing of fact over possibility is not total, of course. We also value creativity in its proper place; corporations invite managers and other employees to "think outside the box" and value creative solutions to recurring problems. Vicariously we can enjoy the surprising change from the expected that comes from seeing a problem in a new way or the unexpected punch line that produces our experiences of humor and laughter. At times, there is even an enchantment with those whose imaginative capacities open up new ways of looking at ourselves or at the world. Even for us adults there is a time and place for the play of creativity.

But the overall ethos in which we live and move and have our being remains that of hardheaded realism. The creativity of the brainstorming session must be tested with focus groups and telephone surveys against the proposal's ultimate impact on the bottom line. We know that it is difficult for individuals, organizations, or communities to survive with their "heads in the clouds." When budgets in schools, businesses, or communities are in crisis, the arts are often the first line item to go. While the arts are surely not the only creations of our imaginations, they may be their purest.

Perception	Memory	Imagination
What is	What was	What could be What could have been
Values accuracy	Values accuracy	Values possibility Sometimes values accuracy
Present	Past	Future or alternative past
Logical	Logical	Logic optional

None of us can survive without our imaginations. It is hard for us to comprehend that our mental and spiritual lives depend as heavily on imagination as they do, that imagination is not an occasional detour from reality but an ongoing process of making sense of the world. The dilemma comes from understanding perception, memory, and imagination as such separate processes. Those images of brilliant sunshine have recalled a lifetime of memories in the sun, drawing us into the pleasure of warmth, the dangers of sunburn, or even beyond our experience to images of blinding light or searing flames.

A Brief, Recent History of Truth

A related concern is our understanding of Pilate's ancient question, "What is truth?" As a result of the Enlightenment dualism spawned by René Descartes, we have separated body from mind, and soul has suffered nearly total neglect. Religion and science parted ways in their competing methodologies for determining truth. The empiricism of the scientific method has produced the technological advances that have extended life and human capabilities astronomically beyond what was possible a few hundred years ago. At the same time, techno-logical advances have come often at the expense of that which cannot be tested by observable measures. If we can't count it, it doesn't exist. In this age of science we have benefited from healthier lives and the availability of immediate communication with others around our planet; at the same time, our needs for connection with self, with others, and with the divine continue frequently unmet. We have the means to communicate but sadly too little to say to each other. We can experience virtual realities in our own homes, but we continue to struggle with racism, human divisions, and war. We are able to perform many tasks at once, but we are not always sure why we are doing them.

The Enlightenment brought with it a conviction of a knowable and manageable reality. Our convictions about how much better off we humans are thanks to the scientific method are deeply held today. Yet into the midst of all of this modernism has crept uneasiness with a sense of the absoluteness of knowable truth. The all too frequent op-pression of others by those who were convinced of their own sense of the truth has contributed to a breakdown of confidence in any single source of truth. Postmodernism has left us with a new skepticism about what truth is attainable by humanity — or more accurately, whether we can even speak of truth.

Emerging discoveries in the brain sciences are offering us new ways to understand the ways our brains operate; the ways they perceive, record, and recall experience; and the intricate relationships between our knowing and our feeling. Indeed, in recent years brain scien-tists have ventured into the arena of human consciousness.[2] What is emerging is a picture of the meaning-making, interpreting brain, far more complicated and sophisticated than any currently conceivable

---

2. See, for example, Antonio Damasio, *The Feeling of What Happens: Body and Emotion in the Making of Consciousness* (New York: Harcourt Brace, 1999); Joseph LeDoux, *Synaptic Self: How Our Brains Become Who We Are* (New York: Viking, 2002); Gerald M. Edelman and Giulio Tononi, *A Universe of Consciousness: How Matter Becomes Imagination* (New York: Basic Books, 2000).

computer and far from the passive receiver of data from its environment we sometimes have imagined it to be. Our brains and our minds (the processes by which our brains operate) are by their very nature constructive, acting upon information fully as much as taking it in. Our brains are constantly creating, and our understanding of the nature of truth is transformed in the process.

The task in this volume is not so much to undermine our trust in our memories or in what we are seeing as it is to blur the distinctions between memory and imagination, to appreciate the deep ways in which perception and memory and imagination belong to each other. In so doing, it should become clear that our care for each other and our experiences of God are expressions of that same meaning-making brain.

It's been a long, hard road as Western civilization has attempted to recover from Descartes's mind/body dualism. We have even further subdivided mind into mind and spirit, embedding our understandings of our self and of others into the three distinct dimensions of body, mind, and spirit. Intuitively, we know all three dimensions influence each other, and we may even comprehend that all three are aspects of the same persons. The last fifty years or so in medicine has witnessed a renewed emphasis on the profound relationship between psyche (mind or soul) and soma (body). Yet we continue to think of ourselves as composed of three separate dimensions and frequently attend to only one or two of those dimensions rather than the whole.

A central message arising from the neurobiological discoveries of recent years recalls us to a more holistic view of persons, acknowledging the embeddedness of mind and spirit in body. Our minds and our spirits are embodied; images of personhood in the Hebrew Scriptures that emphasize the unity of our being turn out to be more contemporary than the tripartite images of recent centuries. Even some of those committed to the Christian church's traditions have argued that the processes we have historically ascribed to the concept of "soul" can now be understood and described on the basis of capacities of the human brain.

Neuropsychologist Warren S. Brown, for instance, argues that soul is "not an essence apart from the physical self, but the net sum of those encounters in which embodied humans relate to and commune with God (who is spirit) or with one another in a manner that reaches deeply into the essence of our creaturely, historical, and communal selves."[3] Paralleling the arguments in this volume, Brown suggests that soul arises out of our capacity for personal relatedness and depends on distinct human abilities such as language, theory of mind, episodic memory, conscious top-down agency, future orientation, and emotional modulation. Our bodies, and particularly the brains accountable for their survival and well-being, are centers of meaning making. We observe our world and ourselves in that world. We relate to ourselves, to each other, and to God through the matrix of capabilities built into our brains.[4]

It is certainly true that our capacity to use our brains does not depend on knowing exactly how they work. In fact, if our brains depended on conscious awareness of each of their functions, we would quickly fail at life's most elementary tasks. Most of the brain's processes are automatic, rapid, and unconscious, resulting in an efficiency that in many situations is life saving. Nonetheless, the more we can learn and absorb about the way in which our meaning-making organ functions, the more fully can we understand our own holistic nature and the more we may be able to inform the practices of our religious communities. Realizing that the brain is first and foremost a monitor of the body, for instance, calls us to think more carefully about the way movement and gesture immediately influence the activity of the brain — the ways we move influence what we think and believe. With that vision in mind, we turn to the first of our three partners — imagination.

3. Warren Brown, Nancey Murphy, and H. Newton Malony, eds., *Whatever Happened to the Soul? Scientific and Theological Portraits of Human Nature* (Minneapolis: Fortress Press, 1998), 101–4.

4. James Ashbrook and Carol Rausch Albright, *The Humanizing Brain: Where Religion and Neuroscience Meet* (Cleveland: Pilgrim Press, 1997); Eugene d'Aquili and Andrew B. Newberg, *The Mystical Mind: Probing the Biology of Religious Experience* (Minneapolis: Fortress Press, 1999).

Imagery

This wonderful and dangerous dimension of our experience deserves a closer look. Let's begin by noting the root of the word imagination, *image*. Image suggests to us a picture or representation of some object. When we look at a snapshot of one of our children, we are certainly not looking at that child himself or herself. We are looking at a piece of paper that has been chemically treated to change colors as it is struck by light. Light once bounced off that child through the lens of a camera onto a film. That film, after appropriate processing, directed similar light patterns onto the paper we hold in our hands, or in our family scrapbook. That image is unable to look back at us, to respond to our look or our words, or to hear anything that we might want to say to it. That image cannot feel our touch, notice our loving smile, or cower under our angry stare. The image is not my Chris or Stephanie or Amy or Lisa.

When we ask a portrait artist to paint a picture of that same child, the image is both further removed from the object and closer to it in an even more striking way. The light rays reflected from my child no longer directly reach the film to be transferred to the paper I am holding. Now the image in front of me has been reflected through a different kind of lens — the eye and hand of the artist — introducing elements of human interpretation and physical execution into the process. An artist may have excellent technical skill with the ability to re-create in the smallest detail and the finest brushstroke the strands of hair, the position of the hands, the color of the eyes. But if she does not see the inner spirit and vitality of my child or catch the poignant sadness in his life, she fails to create a working image. If she is able to plumb the depths of my child's gifts and tragedies, but can't put them to paper or canvas, she fails once again. Both vision and implementation are critical.

Art, of course, varies widely in its desire to represent with precise accuracy the physical characteristics of an object. For many artists, the goal is not one of realism but rather one of interpretation, or even more precisely, the depiction of a truth that lies far beneath the surface of physical appearance. Some art seems to bear little or no physical resemblance to the objects it purports to interpret. But for much of art, the "seeing" is of an aesthetic or spiritual truth that a photograph or "realistic" picture could never capture. In that sense, the painting or sculpture is much closer to the reality of the object than any mechanical picture could ever achieve, or at least comes closer to a different "reality."

Images

An image stands in for the object to which it refers.[5] An image reconstructs recognizable dimensions of the object in another medium — the medium of paper, of canvas, of chemicals, and even of the neural pathways in the brain. We assume the presence of an object — a "real" physical person, place, or thing in the world — and the image we hold in our hand reconstructs and sometimes reinterprets that object.

The word "image" is not limited to paintings and photographs or even to sculptures and drawings. We also create images in our minds, and we do it constantly. The images our brains create of the world and of ourselves are in fact the only real way we have of experiencing the world around us.[6] Here the process becomes even more intriguing, but it is important first to distinguish three building blocks in this process: perception, image, and imagination.

These three building blocks apply to all our senses. We perceive sounds, smells, touches, and tastes as surely as we do sights. And any or all of our senses may be activated in any given encounter. (In chapter 2 we look more closely at how those different senses are recorded and later recalled.) Thus images, including their memories,

---

5. Damasio, *The Feeling of What Happens*, 320–21.
6. Charles D. Laughlin Jr., John McManus, and Eugene G. d'Aquili, *Brain, Symbol and Experience: Toward a Neurophenomenology of Human Consciousness* (New York: Columbia University Press, 1992), 34–75.

are multimodal; that is, they may consist of input from one or several senses at once.[7]

Though we are accustomed to thinking of images as visual representations, the brain records the sounds, smells, textures, and tastes that accompany those sights, or that may signal objects we can't see. Nonetheless, vision is undoubtedly the best understood of the five senses and has received the most research attention, so seeing shall serve as a focus for our reflections.

Perception refers to those psychological and neurological processes by which we take in information about an object in the environment and identify or recognize it. Given that the precise meaning of perception has become diluted in common usage so that it now includes such additional meanings as point of view or opinion, the word "percept" here is used to refer to the content and the result of the process of perception. *Imagery* refers to the internal pictures (or recollections of sounds or smells) that the brain creates and stores and that it then uses in identifying similar objects in the future. *Imagination* includes the mind/brain's creative capacity to make changes in images and organize them in stories to interpret the world around us.

We know the basics of the perception process. I come home from work and walk into the family room. Someone is sitting on the sofa reading. Particular light patterns strike the retina of my eye where they stimulate the firing of neurons, which send signals to the thalamus in the middle of my brain and then on to the back of my brain — the occipital area. And there it gets interesting. Our brains use some neurons to study the shapes of objects and others to determine their outlines as the brain momentarily struggles to figure out what it is seeing. Still other neurons determine whether the object is standing still or moving. Yet others provide a sense of orientation or spatial relationships — where we stand in relationship to the object of our attention. The brain then puts these bits of information

---

7. Damasio, *The Feeling of What Happens,* 318.

together in successive stages (in what are called "association areas" or "convergence zones") to form a whole picture.

How the brain actually puts together these discrete qualities of an object into a coherent whole is known by neuroscientists as "the binding problem." Each sensory system (visual, auditory, etc.) integrates the discrete dimensions (referred to as "qualia") specific to that sense; then the brain further integrates the productions of the various sensory systems into a percept. The final integration appears to take place in the prefrontal cortex.[8] That's the *input* side of the process.

Active Looking

But my brain is not just taking in information. At the very instant my brain begins receiving information it starts to interpret. This process involves a kind of template stored in the brain—general schemas or maps that the brain uses in recognizing and identifying an object. The brain appears to have general pictures of particular categories of objects, such as dogs, people, or rocks. Neuroscientists continue to have significant disagreement about the exact nature or location of these internal schemas. Nevertheless, the brain is remarkably adept, even at a very young age, at distinguishing between the ancient "animal, vegetable, or mineral" categories of objects in the world, or more specifically animal, person, tool, natural object, and plant.[9] Those categories become even more differentiated as the brain continues to develop and as experience further informs the growing child.

When we are receiving information from outside us through our eyes, our brain immediately begins matching that input with one of these templates. It is actually sending pictures back down the pipeline and asking, "Is it this?" "Do these two fit together?" "Do we have a match?" So at the same instant that light from this person in my family room strikes my eyeball, my brain begins sending out pictures to determine a match. And here the two sides of my brain help me

8. LeDoux, *Synaptic Self*, 193–95.
9. Pascal Boyer, *Religion Explained* (New York: Basic Books, 2001), 78.

in different ways. The right hemisphere takes in the big picture — it knows that I am in my own house and is aware that I am not alone. My right brain might not have many words for what it is seeing, but it is busy scanning the room for an overall impression. My left brain is a bit more interested in the details, and it eventually will be able to give me words for what I am seeing.[10]

My brain has ways of selecting certain images out of the many that bombard it at any given time. The brain particularly and automatically focuses its attention on movement, novelty, familiarity, or perhaps on something that ancestors from many generations before have discovered could be dangerous, such as snakes — like those that are reported in unwanted abundance in southern Arizona during these spring months while I am writing. The brain comes prepackaged with some images that it finds significant; others it learns from experience to love or fear. Increasingly, research is demonstrating that the brain makes appraisals even of images it cannot yet consciously identify. On a walk through the woods I might see a long thin object beside the path and eventually recognize it as a fallen tree branch. But my brain may already have registered the image as a potential threat — a snake — so that my heart is pounding and my breathing labored until my conscious brain reassures the body that all is well. As we note later, the brain actually has different systems for thinking and feeling. In fact, unconscious or subliminal images may provoke emotional responses more readily than those of which we are aware.[11]

For whatever combination of reasons, in my own living room my brain has already figured out that there is an object across the room from me even before I can identify it. It probably has detected some slight movement, which tells me this is not a rock — a helpful beginning. It next narrows the possibilities to a human being and finally to a woman. We're getting closer now. But in my house, at this moment

10. Robert Ornstein, *The Right Mind* (New York: Harcourt Brace, 1997), 108.

11. Joseph LeDoux, *The Emotional Brain: The Mysterious Underpinnings of Emotional Life* (New York: Touchstone, 1996), 59.

in time, this still leaves me three possibilities. My brain knows I need to figure this out and do it quickly. So it narrows the range of details I am looking at. Now I need to know something about hair color. If it's brown rather than blonde, I've eliminated one possibility. But it could still be my wife or our seventeen-year-old Amy. My brain narrows the search even further. At last it recognizes the book in this woman's hand as an exegesis of the Gospel of John. It's my wife! We have a match. Now I know whether to expect a hug and possible discussion of theology rather than a brief smile or grunt and a request for help with homework.

Fortunately it does not take my brain nearly as long to accomplish this task as it does to try to describe it. I'd be in big trouble otherwise. In a nanosecond, my brain took into account where I was, distinguished between living and nonliving objects, and narrowed my search to reassure me that this was the person I was most hoping to see when I came home. It helped my brain immensely, of course, that this was what I was *expecting* to see. And what I am expecting to see is also then colored by my history with that person. I am anticipating warmth and affection rather than a frightened burglar running out the back door.

But the point of it all is this: from the instant we begin looking at something or someone, our brains are interpreting what we are seeing. The brain is seeking a match by sending out pictures of what this object could be.[12] If the brain sees something it has never seen before, particularly if it looks inviting or dangerous, the brain struggles mightily to figure out what the image is — to fit it into categories that are ready at hand. The brain is making educated guesses about what's really out there. We may become aware of this usually unconscious and rapid process when our brain "stumbles" and we struggle to recall someone we've seen before but just can't quite place. Our brains do not just passively receive what the outside world is offering us. We're making interpretations of our perceptions all the time. We

---

12. Stephen M. Kosslyn, *Image and Brain: The Resolution of the Imagery Debate* (Cambridge, Mass.: MIT Press, 1994), 73–74.

are creating images and matching images every time we look or listen or touch or taste. Our brains are natural interpreters.

In this sense, our images are more like art than snapshots. We are not merely having chemical reactions to light, sound, or textures. Our brains are first selecting what objects in the world we will pay closer attention to. We have to be selective, given the overwhelming number of things that could attract our attention. We cannot attend to everything, of course. Some things are in the foreground while others are in the background. Our brains do this automatically. Mine, for instance, certainly recognizes my wife Diane on the couch. Should a football game be on the television at the same time, my brain will face a dilemma. Its automatic first response would be to identify the teams and the score, while the better part of me knows I should be paying closer attention to the woman with whom I share my life. Sometimes the will must override the brain's automatic processes.

To be more precise, the brain processes mental images in stages, beginning with gross depictions in the primary (or first) visual cortex at the back of the brain. Those early steps in the process do reconstruct the visually perceived object in geographic patterns in the cortex; that is, they are "mapped" onto the brain in such a way that a crudely recognizable pattern of the object could be detected if one could highlight the neurons that are active at the moment of attentive gazing.[13]

Yet as those signals travel "up" the visual systems in the brain, the patterns become less and less detectable by simply lighting up the neurons that are being activated. The brain's association areas are doing just what their name implies — they are connecting the distinct dimensions of objects into a coherent whole, resulting in what the mind registers as a percept. From the very beginning of the process, the brain is actually sending educated guesses back "down" the pipeline for at least two separate purposes: first, to focus visual

---

13. Steven Pinker, *How the Mind Works* (New York: W. W. Norton, 1997), 287.

attention on particular objects or parts of objects in order to improve identification recognition, and second, to identify the object specifically.

Images Conscious and Unconscious

We have already noted that images are more than visual pictures; images contain the sounds, smells, textures, and tastes with which we experience them. Images are multimodal. In addition, many of our images are beyond our awareness. They are operating constantly and usually unobtrusively. If images are the "currency of our minds,"[14] then many more images are operating at any one time than we could ever hold in conscious awareness.

This world of the unconscious is indeed a controversial one. Behavioral and cognitive theorists see little evidence for an unconscious mind and concentrate instead on persons' explicit thoughts and behaviors. But among theorists who do posit a significant, powerful force to affects and cognitions of which we are generally unaware, the unconscious is understood in at least two different ways. Sigmund Freud and the psychodynamic theorists who followed him contend that a vast arena of human thought and emotion drives an individual's thinking, feeling, and behavior. This arena of emotional life consists of repressed and suppressed memories to which one gains access primarily through dreams, slips of the tongue, and psychodynamic therapies. Carl Jung expanded the notion of the unconscious to include the accumulated experiences of the human species: the collective unconscious.

Cognitive neuroscientists describe an unconscious of a different sort. Steven Pinker, Pascal Boyer, and Michael Gazzaniga, among others, posit a limited range of mental processes constantly at work in mental life which operate in the "basement of the mind." Rather than consisting of repressed memories, however, these processes consist of

---

14. Damasio, *The Feeling of What Happens*, 319.

inherited mechanisms, sometimes called "modules," with which evolution has endowed human brains. These mental mechanisms evolved to solve particular types of problems that are critical to survival, like a fear response which protects us from potential danger, or the ability to recognize faces and evaluate their intentions toward us. In this sense, these mechanisms are unconscious in much the same way that we are not usually conscious of our own heartbeat, respiration, or the contraction of individual muscles, unless we have just completed our first full workout in six months. We become aware of them when they hurt, when they are working at full tilt, or when they simply stop working.

For our purposes, however, it is sufficient to acknowledge that the brain/mind operates with a "teeming cauldron" of images at any given moment, that these images don't stand still, and that we may be conscious of only a fraction of them at any one time. What is often at stake is which of them we choose to notice or which ones virtually thrust themselves upon us.

Brain's Body, Body's Brain

Images clearly have both external and internal sources. The world around us is full of sensory signals at any moment, bombarding our eyes, ears, noses, and bodies, and therefore, ultimately our brains as well. And from moment to moment, many more signals become available as the world changes. If that weren't enough incoming information, the brain also is constantly receiving signals from the body itself. The brain is constantly "observing" the body's own posture, general emotional tone, and external boundaries.[15] The information channels include direct neuron connections from the body to an area of the brain's parietal lobe known as the somatosensory cortex, as well as from chemicals it detects in the bloodstream.

---

15. Antonio Damasio, *Descartes' Error: Emotion, Reason, and the Human Brain* (New York: G. P. Putnam's Sons, 1994), 226–35.

Neuroscientists a long time ago discarded the notion of a "little person" in the brain. Unlike the small man in the Wizard of Oz, operating this body/mind from somewhere deep within, there is no "cockpit" in the brain occupied by a miniature pilot. Instead, this complex organ called the brain is involved in its entirety in monitoring our bodies and the worlds our bodies inhabit. In fact, as we shall see later, while recording the presence of the object, the brain is simultaneously recording its own posture and relationship to that object, all of which is then recorded in memory.[16] This fact has real significance when we discuss memory in chapter 2 and worship and other religious experiences in chapters 4 and 6. Small wonder that our minds can manage only a tiny percentage of all that information at any particular moment, and by far the vast majority of the images present in our brains remains hidden from view.

Attention

This small window of images available to our consciousness at any point in time varies widely in both size and focus. Some scientists go so far as to define consciousness as the window of attention that is regularly expanding and narrowing. When we're concerned about nothing in particular, and not concentrating on a given task or object at hand, the window is a wide one. More precisely, the window plays over the landscape without fixing on any particular image. Enter some disturbing event, like a piercing scream from down the hall or the sudden recollection of a meeting I was to have attended thirty minutes ago, and suddenly my attention becomes narrowly fixed. It's as though something inside me or outside me is jumping up and down, hand waving furiously in the air, frantically calling out, "Hey, over here! Look at me! I need you." Of course, my reverie may be disturbed just as quickly by an appealing occurrence, such as an

---

16. Damasio, *The Feeling of What Happens,* 147–48.

invitation to lunch with my wife or a phone call suggesting I quit work early today and attend a ball game with a friend.

Attention may sometimes serve the will, but that is far from certain. I may choose to keep my attention focused on the words I am now writing (with varying degrees of success) or concentrate on a play or concert. At other times, my brain may seem to have a mind of its own and obsessively fix on some object I would really rather not be thinking about at all, at least at this moment.

A Brief (De)tour through the Brain

We've waited as long as we can to describe the brain itself; the time has come. For the purposes of our discussion throughout the rest of this volume we need some familiarity with the basic structures of the brain for our own reference. (For readers already familiar with the anatomy of the brain, or those who don't like drawings of the brain, feel free to skip ahead a couple of pages. For those who just don't like the technical stuff, hang with me; I'll try to make this as brief and painless as possible.)

Viewed from the outside (minus the protective skull of course) the brain is a roundish three-pound mass of gray and white matter, looking for all the world like a map of the moon with all its bumps and grooves. This lump of tissue is divided into two roughly equal hemispheres on the right and left side. The visible outside of the brain is called the cortex, or more commonly the *neocortex,* referring to the conviction that this structure was the most recent evolutionary development in the brain (see the diagram of the cerebral cortex on p. 31). The neocortex envelops nearly all the other structures of the brain; this is what we would see if we were to remove the brain from the skull. It is the seat of most of our higher cognitive functions, including logic, problem solving, intuitive psychology, and our sense of the passage of time.

Each hemisphere is divided into four sections or lobes, each of which plays critical roles in particular dimensions of mental life. At

Cerebral Cortex

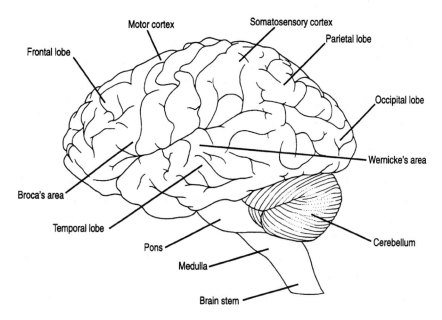

the front of the brain is the appropriately named *frontal lobe,* which is vital in planning, forethought, regulation of social interaction, and empathy. Not surprisingly, the frontal lobes are proportionally much larger in human beings than in any other mammal; we are much more capable of the processes we now know that those tissues support — functions vital to living in a social world and to the processes of imagination itself.

Directly behind the frontal lobe and near the top of the brain lies the *parietal lobe.* This brain section, nestled comfortably in between the other three lobes, plays critical roles in pulling together or associating input from those sources. Among other functions, damage to the parietal lobes of the brain can interfere with the brain's ability to orient itself in space. Recognizing faces is also supported by the right parietal lobe.

Directly below the parietal lobe is the *temporal lobe*, located just inside each ear. Not surprisingly, this section of the brain not only supports hearing and language; it is critical for long-term memory. The fourth and final lobe of the brain lies directly at the back and is known as the *occipital lobe*. The primary visual cortex is located here, and damage in this area results in various visual disturbances. The small round bulb at the lower back of the brain is called the *cerebellum;* among other functions it appears to be critical in maintaining balance and coordination and in focusing attention.

So much for the outside of the brain. If we separate our theoretical model of the brain right down the middle, we can get a view of its internal structures. The brain can be thought of as having three separate sections. The bumpy outer layer we've already described is the neocortex. Below the cortex (hence, "subcortically") lie a number of structures that play key roles in the regulation of emotion, nurturing behavior, and management of memory. The structures together have commonly been referred to as the *limbic system,* though as neuroscientists learn more of the functions of various structures of the brain there is less inclination to think of these structures as an isolated subsystem within the brain.

Located directly beneath the cortex and limbic system and on the top of the spinal column is the *brain stem.* What looks like an enlargement or bulb at the end of the spinal cord actually contains structures that are responsible for the maintenance of life itself, including blood pressure, heart rate, and respiration. The brain stem is also responsible for managing the body's general state of arousal and attentiveness.

Between the neocortex and the brain stem, and linking the two half brains together, is a band of several million neurons, collectively known as the *corpus callosum.* (This is the structure that was surgically cut in certain severely epileptic patients, all in an effort to keep epileptic seizures that began on one side of the brain from traveling to the other. The operations were quite successful in limiting the impact of the seizures; studies of these patients by Dr. Roger Sperry

Internal Structures of the Brain

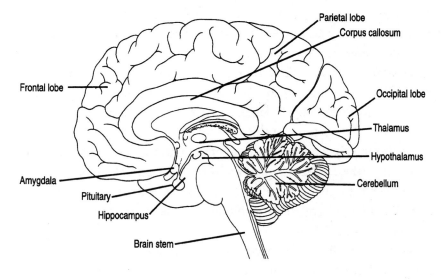

and cohorts following the surgeries led to the profound discoveries of the different functions of the left and right hemispheres in the human brain, and the consequences of severing their primary communication channels. But more about that in chapter 3.)

Of particular importance to us here are four small clusters of nerve cells that play important functions in imagination and memory. The *hippocampus,* from the Greek term for "seahorse," is particularly known for the role it plays in consolidating long-term memory. The *thalamus,* to which we referred above in the brief narrative of my recognition of my wife, is an important relay station from the sensory organs to the cortex, as well as to other brain structures. Immediately below the thalamus is the aptly named *hypothalamus,* which plays critical roles in emotion. And last, but by no means least, is the *amygdala,* from the Greek for "almond," a close if not perfect metaphor. The amygdala plays a key role in the fear system of the brain.

The Triune Brain

Neurophysiologist Paul MacLean carefully considered the potential implications of these three sections of the brain as signs of evolutionary development. The most extensive synthesis of his work appeared in *The Triune Brain in Evolution,* published in 1990. He believed that the brain stem contained structures very similar to those of primitive creatures like reptiles. He labeled this structure therefore the "reptilian" brain. Structures of the limbic system (a term that he coined) correlated nicely with structures in other mammals; hence he referred to them as the "paleomammalian" (or old mammal) brain. Finally, recognizing the higher cognitive functions attributable to the outer cortex in humans and other primates, he labeled this structure as the "neomammalian" brain.

This "triune brain" theory profoundly influenced the way neuroscientists have thought about the brain since the middle of the last century. The elegant architecture of the model lends itself quite nicely to correlations with certain specific Christian theological understandings of God. James Ashbrook and Carol Rausch Albright, for instance, explored images of God as evidenced in the functioning of the tripartite brain.[17] Our brains, as part of the universe, serve as a bridge between religious consciousness and the universe itself, providing clues to the underlying structure of the world. They argued that the human brain has evolved to make sense of its environment, and the way it does so is to see in the universe (and God) qualities of the brain itself. So the brain "humanizes" the world around it; and those human attributes the brain perceives mirror the world's own qualities because the brain is part of that universe. In the reptilian brain, responsible for arousal and alertness, Ashbrook and Albright find sources (and reflections) of a watchful, ever-present God. In the limbic system, credited with emotion and caregiving, they find a nurturing God. The neocortex reflects an organizing God and in the

---

17. Ashbrook and Albright, *The Humanizing Brain.*

frontal lobes, seat of planning and intention, they find images of a purposeful God.

One of the dilemmas with MacLean's theory today is that it suggests three separate brains that, despite their functional separation, find ways to work together. Evolutionary neurobiologists now emphasize that, as the evolving human brain developed newer, more advanced structures, the function and structure of the earlier forms of the brain themselves were irrevocably changed and integrated into the new brain.[18] In addition, some species such as birds and reptiles turn out to have the equivalent of neocortical tissues as well. This discovery may undermine at least a literal interpretation of the neocortex as "new mammalian."[19]

Before we tire of our brief anatomy lesson, let us return to our discussion of images and imagination. (If you tuned out, or skipped over the geography lesson, this would be a good time to rejoin us.)

Images and Feelings

So far we have spoken of images as though they are neutral digital images recorded on a computer's hard drive. For the kinds of images with which we are concerned here, however, quite the opposite is true. We've already noted that the brain is far from a passive receiver of information. Instead, the brain very carefully selects the particular stimuli to which it will respond and orients the body itself in such a way as to maximize that attention, at the same time screening out irrelevant data.

But how does the brain make those instantaneous decisions? Of all that buzzing chaos of stimuli out there, how does the brain choose what is most important? Even the fastest computer we can imagine would take far too long calculating all the possibilities when it observes a car careening toward it on a sidewalk.

---

18. Pinker, *How the Mind Works*, 370–72.
19. LeDoux, *Synaptic Self*, 35.

Here the power and purpose of emotion and feelings become evident.[20] Our brains are hardwired to respond automatically to certain types of events in the world and to overlook others. Movement, novelty, other persons, pain, fear, and expectation all attract our attention even before our conscious minds can register their presence, let alone identify them. In fact, we are much more likely to attend to objects that could hurt us than we are to those that promise to give us pleasure. When you think about it, our brains are really pretty wise, knowing that we will live a lot longer by avoiding things that could kill us even if we run the risk of missing out on some opportunities for a little fun. Our brains truly seem to operate on a better-safe-than-sorry premise.

Many of the images our brains record, then, are automatically tagged with an emotional label, alerting us grossly to whether we want to approach this object in the environment or run away as fast as we can. In fact, the brain has two separate systems for registering the presence of important objects in the environment. One neural circuit operates very rapidly, yet gives us only a very general idea about the desirability of this new experience. What the brain gains in speed, it loses in precision. The brain is making a snap decision about whether to race to embrace this object or run away like the dickens. Neuroscientist Joseph LeDoux convincingly describes this "fear system" and emphasizes the role of the amygdala (that small almond-shaped structure in the very center of the brain) and its connections to various sensory and body-monitoring brain structures.[21]

An emotional stimulus triggers a signal on a direct pathway to the sensory thalamus in the middle of the brain. From there those signals branch both to the sensory cortex and to the amygdala; the amygdala has neuronal connections with the hypothalamus, which initiates a release of stress hormones into the bloodstream, and quickly at that. The pathway from the thalamus to the amygdala is the shorter circuit,

---

20. Daniel Goleman, *Emotional Intelligence* (New York: Bantam Books, 1995); Damasio, *Descartes' Error*; LeDoux, *The Emotional Brain.*
21. LeDoux, *The Emotional Brain.*

preparing the organism to flee or fight. The pathway through the sensory cortex and back to the amygdala is longer and therefore takes more time — all in order to be more discriminating and precise. This second parallel system goes to work at the same time but takes longer to get to its result. This system is able to identify much more precisely what the object is and what action the organism expediently should take toward it. The brain has traded speed for precision.

What is critical for our purposes here is the fact that, at least as far as it concerns the fear system that underlies our human experience of anxiety, two very different brain pathways appear to be responsible for detecting and recording thoughts and feelings — at least feelings of fear. As we shall see in chapter 2, these two different dimensions of memories are stored separately in the brain. This mechanism of learning to flee, fight, or approach is hardwired and present even before birth. But we also learn from our experiences, and over time, we develop a large repertoire of scenarios that can produce automatic preconscious responses.

Emotion and Reason

Making sharp distinctions between thoughts and feelings is far from something new. Psychotherapists from their earliest training are taught to pay close attention to the differences and particularly to demonstrate interest in feelings over thoughts. "Tell me how you feel about that, not what you think about it," is a frequently heard directive in many counseling sessions.

One of the reasons, of course, that counselors attend to feelings so carefully is that North American culture has historically valued thinking much more highly than its emotional counterparts. Feelings are generally understood to cloud judgment, to interfere with rational problem-solving skills, and to result in sentimental, irrational choices. The single most important icon in this regard has been the IQ score or intelligence quotient.

What is emerging in the last several decades from educational psychologists, cognitive scientists, and neurology is an appreciation for the critical role that emotion plays in intelligent living. Psychologist Daniel Goleman has coined the term "emotional intelligence" to underscore these discoveries,[22] and Harvard psychologist Howard Gardner and others have broadened categories of intelligence even further by referring to "multiple intelligences," adding to the traditional intelligence categories of language, logic, and mathematics such categories as bodily-kinesthetic, spatial, musical, interpersonal, and intrapersonal intelligences.[23]

An early dramatic example of this profound connection is the increasingly familiar story of Phineas Gage as described by neurologist Antonio Damasio.[24] The action took place in 1848 New England, where Gage, by all accounts an affable and efficient supervisor, was overseeing a group of men laying track for the Rutland & Burlington Railroad. When he was distracted momentarily from his work of setting explosives, tragically the explosives ignited and a thirteen-pound, three-and-a-half-foot tamping rod was driven upward through Gage's left cheek and out the top of his skull. Miraculously Gage survived and within a couple of months was declared "cured." It was clear that his language and general problem-solving skills were unaffected.

But as time went by, it became clearer that this was not the same Phineas Gage. He was unable to hold a job, his language became crude, and he was unable to make decisions that were in his own best interests, let alone the interests of others. He could no longer act in accordance with social norms for behavior. In short, he had undergone a dramatic personality change that was directly the result of this dramatic neurological trauma. He wandered around the country, including a stint in South America, finally settling with his

---

22. Goleman, *Emotional Intelligence.*
23. Howard Gardner, *Frames of Mind: The Theory of Multiple Intelligences* (New York: Basic Books, 1983).
24. Damasio, *Descartes' Error,* 3–33.

family in San Francisco, where he died unnoticed in 1861 at the age of thirty-eight following severe epileptic seizures.

Approximately 120 years later, neuroscientists Hannah Damasio, Albert Galaburda, and Thomas Grabowski obtained Gage's skull and through current MRI techniques were able to determine the exact brain locations that were damaged by the exploding rod. They determined the specific areas of the prefrontal cortex that had been damaged and confirmed that Gage's accident had left language and motor areas intact, while destroying sections of the brain that we now know contribute to conscience, empathy, and care of self.[25]

It is important for our purposes here to note that while key intellectual and emotional capacities appear to be located in particular areas of the brain, our effective functioning depends on the work of the whole brain, not just particular functions that had been associated with narrowly defined types of intelligence. Further, while linear thinking and problem solving and their connections with language are critical functions, they cannot operate effectively in the world without the humanizing functions of emotion and feeling. In fact, judgment, conscience, and care require the forward-looking, empathizing functions of the frontal lobes every bit as much as they require the logical functions of the left neocortex.

Antonio Damasio has developed this concept most elaborately in his description of the "somatic marker device."[26] Reasoning requires that we analyze a wide range of imagined scenarios and outcomes constructed by our imaging brains. Each scenario prompts a body-based (somatic) response which biases us either toward or away from that possibility, thus limiting the number of alternatives to a manageable number. Some of the most complex decisions we make occur in social situations, and they must be made quickly — an advantage of the brain's emotional processing. Poor Phineas Gage lost the guidance

25. Hannah Damasio, Thomas Grabowski, Randall Frank, Albert M. Galaburda, and Antonio R. Damasio, "The Return of Phineas Gage: Clues About the Brain from the Skull of a Famous Patient," *Science,* New Series, 264, no. 5162 (May 20, 1994): 1102–5.
26. Damasio, *Descartes' Error,* 165–201.

of his somatic marker device and, along with it, his capacity for good judgment. Pure reason without emotion is not only inefficient, it may even be bankrupt.

Imaging the Other—Empathy and the Brain

We human beings, even more than our primate cousins, live as much in a social world as we do in a physical world. Our survival depends on our abilities to communicate with others, to understand their experiences (to know who is friend and who is foe), and to offer mutual protection and care. It will come as no surprise to discover that the human brain has evolved sophisticated methods enhancing our abilities to navigate the sometimes treacherous waters of social relationships. Entering into the experience of another's distress is not just a matter of our humanness; empathy is the ground from which relationships of care grow.

Our capacity for viewing the world through another's eyes is grounded in the structures of the brain. And we are not alone. Since at least the 1960s, neuroscientists and comparative psychologists have noticed that humans are not the only species who give evidence of empathic responses to other distressed members of their species. An albino rat, in one famous experiment, views another being hoisted in a sling and presses a bar so that he is lowered again to the ground. Rhesus monkeys will literally starve themselves rather than pull a chain that would give them food but shock another rhesus monkey. Members of many species experience distress as they see the distress of another and act to stop that distress even at their own risk.[27]

Because empathy in human beings involves a complex constellation of capacities such as selection and attention, working memory,

---

27. G. E. J. Rice and P. Gainer, "'Altruism' in the Albino Rat," *Journal of Comparative and Physiological Psychology* 55 (1962): 123–25; J. H. Masserman, S. Wechkin, W. Terris, "'Altruistic' Behavior in Rhesus Monkeys," *American Journal of Psychiatry* 121 (1964): 584–85; reported in Stephanie Preston and Frans B. M. de Waal, "Empathy: Its Ultimate and Proximate Bases," *Behavioral and Brain Sciences* 25 (February 2002): 1–20.

introspection, maintaining a separate sense of self, and a repertoire of helping skills, that empathy draws on diverse areas of the brain is not surprising. Researchers utilizing PET scans and functional magnetic resonance imaging (fMRI) can now detect discrete areas of the brain that support basic functions, such as taking the perspective of another. In one recent study, subjects were asked to imagine an action from two different perspectives — first, when they imagined performing the action themselves, and second, when they imagined someone else performing the same action.[28]

The same regions in the frontal cortex (the premotor regions immediately in front of the brain's central groove, or sulcus) were activated whether they imagined themselves or another performing the task. The two perspectives involved different regions as well: in the first-person scenario, the brain utilized the somatosensory cortex which receives feedback from the position and posture of the body; in the third-person scenario the parietal cortex (which is critical in differentiating self from others) became active, as did the right prefrontal cortex. So at least when we are imagining body movements, our own or others, the brain automatically and unconsciously rehearses the movement as though it is performing the act itself and then draws the distinction between self and other as a way to understand the experience of the other.

In 2001 researchers at the University of Iowa Hospitals used PET imaging to compare brain structures active in emotionally empathic experiences.[29] Subjects were asked to remember and imagine an emotional experience from their own past (fear or anger) and then to recall and imagine an experience of the same emotion from someone else's past. Identical brain structures were found to participate

---

28. Perrine Ruby and Jean Decety, "Effect of Subjective Perspective Taking During Simulation of Action: A PET Investigation of Agency," *Nature Neuroscience* 4, no. 5 (May 2001): 546–50.

29. Stephanie D. Preston, Antoine Bechara, Thomas J. Grabowski, Hannah Damasio, and Antonio R. Damasio. "A Perception-Action Model of Cognitive Empathy? A PET Investigation of Imagining Your Own Experience and Someone Else's," University of Iowa Hospitals and Clinics; Department of Neurology, Iowa City, Iowa, 2002.

in those experiences whether subjects were imagining the events happening to them or to someone else. Such findings lend support to the notion that empathy is, at least in part, "trying on" the experience of another and utilizing our own experiences to understand those of another.

There is a further exciting possibility — that the human brain is constructed in such a way that it automatically "catches" the emotional state of others, especially those in distress. Certain "mirror" neurons have been detected that spontaneously re-create the emotional experience of another even before conscious awareness of that event is available to the empathizer.[30] The phrase "emotional contagion" captures the essence of this interpersonal communication of fear or anxiety. Children are particularly susceptible to the feelings of significant others and begin to develop emotional self-regulation within the context of relationships with parents.

As the frontal regions of the brain develop further and the child gains experience with others and with self, the child learns to inhibit the unrestricted experience of anxiety. One of the exciting implications from these findings is the discovery that our capacities to relate to each other in empathic, caring ways are built into the very structures of our brains.

Active Imagination

We're still quite some distance from what we normally think of when we use the word "imagination." We now take another step from image to imagination. Our brains are built to create and play with images. When a particular area of the brain is not receiving input from the outside, it generates images out of the random signals that are bouncing around in there. Some of those images pop up sponta-

---

30. G. di Pellegrino, L. Fadiga, L. Fogassi, V. Gallese, and G. Rizzolatti, "Understanding Motor Events: A Neurophysiological Study," *Experimental Brain Research* 91 (1992): 176–80; reported in Preston and de Waal, "Empathy: Its Ultimate and Proximate Bases," 17.

neously, while we can choose others. This distinction between images and the objects out there in the real world is critical to our discussion. Once we have the pictures, we are free to play with them in new and unexpected ways.

Planning a dinner party is an exercise in imaginative construction. Our images of the persons we will invite, perhaps selected from a list of potential candidates, pass through our minds and we picture ourselves conversing with them. Memories of past experiences, both consciously remembered and unconscious, trigger both emotional and cognitive associations. We try to imagine who will get along well and how we can avoid having one person dominate the conversation or, even worse, having no one present who has a word to say. We picture guests interacting with each other; we discard one couple and add another in their place. All these steps are imaginative scenarios that would be impossible (or at the very least extremely rude) to accomplish in person.

Imagination has been described and understood in a variety of ways. For our purposes, we shall think of the imagination as made up of the building blocks of images. But now, instead of connecting those pictures to things out there in the real world, the mind can make changes in them. We can turn them upside down or turn them around. We can look at them from any imaginable perspective. We can change their color or shape. We can replace them with other images. We can even take a group of images and put them together in different ways. Now we have freed the mind from any demands that our internal pictures match their outside counterparts. Loosed from the requirement that inside match outside, we can create new pictures out of the raw material of the old pictures.

When we are observing an object in the environment, we are perceiving. Once we have captured the sights, sounds, and smells of that object, our brains have created an image, and now the human brain's unique capacities to play can take center stage. At the simplest level, the brain can take its image of a building and look at it from many different perspectives. We can look at a room in the house and imagine it in a very different paint color or with very different furnishings (though brains obviously vary in their capacity to do this). Some brains appear to be more field-bound than others, more enslaved to what is rather than open to what could be. Nevertheless, brains by their very structures have the capacity to create and reshape images they take in.

Yet restructuring objects we have seen is only the simplest form of imagination. The human brain is capable of much more. Indeed the brain can imagine whole configurations of objects, or even whole stories, and operate on them with some of the same brain mechanisms it uses internally to deal with perceived objects. The brain can take multiple perspectives, tell multiple stories, and think through the consequences of multiple scenarios.

Imagination Reconsidered

So far we have spoken of images primarily as representations of objects in the environment. Yet we also know that the brain uses images to represent other realities as well. The brain's rich association areas connect images that our conscious minds might never consider. Most of us in religious and psychotherapeutic communities stand in a long tradition of careful attentiveness to the symbolic meaning of images and dreams. We have experienced truth revealed through images, both expected and surprising. We find our discussion of those meanings further deepened as we explore memory in chapter 2 and story in chapter 3.

So we define imagination in this way:

Imagination is the distinctively human capacity to envision multiple alternative realities, scenarios, and outcomes. It involves the ability to represent, internally and symbolically, scenarios and configurations of space and time that are not immediately represented to the senses.

Imagination frees us from the tyranny of the present, of the logical, of the "real." It also frees us from the constraints of the now, as it pictures what events were like in the historic past or what they might become in the future.

Let's look more closely at our definition. Undoubtedly, the most significant difference between our brain and the brains of our evolutionary predecessors is this capacity for imagination. All other species are essentially enslaved to the present — the sights, sounds, and smells with which they are confronted at this very moment. At least a primitive memory of sorts is present in, and informs the behavior of, all other living matter. Evolution has equipped many creatures with behaviors that anticipate or prepare for the future, like squirrels storing food for the coming winter. But the capacity to imagine several alternative scenarios at once, to write several potential distinct plot lines at the same time and explore their consequences, appears to be a uniquely human capacity.

There is good reason for this set of circumstances. We human beings are born essentially instinct poor. Our responses to many novel or dangerous situations do not come naturally to us. We have to make many more choices and learn many more skills of living than any other species. But what our evolved brains have offered us instead of a rich repertoire of instincts is a much larger capacity for responding to varying and novel situations. Those large, bumpy brain surfaces known as the neocortex make possible the "theater of consciousness" on which we play out many make-believe possibilities. As we explore more fully in chapter 3, we are constantly writing stories about what is happening, what has happened, and what could happen. It's all a necessary part of our living as human beings. The giftedness of being human is also its own burden.

So the images that inhabit our minds right now have at least three sources (see the diagram on p. 46). Our minds are forming images of this book, of the room where we're sitting. We *perceive* the persons, places, and things that are within our reach or that stand in our

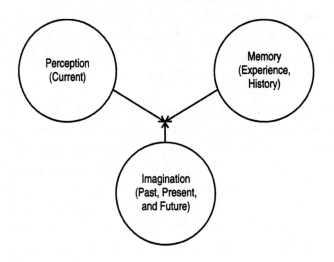

line of vision or that are within earshot right now — the objects we can see, touch, and feel. We also get images from our *memories,* both recent and long past — people we have known, experiences we recall, stories we have been told. And finally, we can create new images out of the old images — things that we have never encountered in the real world, and most of which we never will.

Is It Live, or Is It Memorex?

The brain uses virtually the same mechanisms and processes for images that come from any one of the three sources of perception, memory, or imagination.[31] Once the image gets from the eye to the back of the brain, the brain treats that image in roughly the same way that it does a picture from memory or even one that is made up. After all, it is not a full-blown picture that comes from the eye to the brain anyway; it is a series of nerve impulses that the brain still has to interpret. It doesn't become a picture until the brain turns it into a picture.

---

31. Kosslyn, *Image and Brain,* 54–60.

Whether I am looking at my wife, remembering the last time I saw her this morning, or creating a whole new picture of her, my brain treats that picture in the same manner. In a way, once my brain has an image inside, it can "forget," or perhaps stop caring about, whether that picture is real, remembered, or imaginary.

One of the implications of this state of affairs is, of course, that the human brain (and the body that houses it) can have a difficult time distinguishing between what is "real," what is remembered, and what is imagined.[32] The brain can well experience a memory or an imagined scenario with the same conviction of reality as it can of standing in the presence of an object looking at it in real time. We all have experienced sweaty palms or a pounding heart with the simplest memory of an embarrassing situation, and that can happen even when we *know* we're remembering that event. We can tremble with fright at the mere thought of an IRS audit or a sudden car accident. We can feel our bodies relax or sense a smile on our faces when we anticipate a reunion with a lover or friend — even when there is no such visit on the horizon. Virtual reality — our capacity to feel as though we are actually flying an airplane or fighting space aliens on our computer — depends on this capacity of the brain.

Once our brain grabs hold of an image, it communicates the consequences of that picture to our whole body. It is the reason we are advised to imagine a calm, peaceful lake, a sandy warm beach, or an open green meadow when we are feeling stress. If we can hold those pictures long enough and allow our minds to wrap themselves up in those calming pictures, the body communicates peace and relaxation to the rest of the body, even changing the messenger chemicals within. Perhaps this is one reason Paul cautioned the early Christians to focus their own images on "whatever is true, whatever is honorable, whatever is just, whatever is pure, whatever is pleasing, whatever is commendable, if there is any excellence

---

32. Daniel L. Schacter, ed., *Memory Distortion: How Minds, Brains, and Societies Reconstruct the Past* (Cambridge, Mass.: Harvard University Press, 1995), 23.

and if there is anything worthy of praise, think about these things"
(Phil 4:8).

But Are They Really the Same?

Most of the time we do know the difference between images and
reality, and people who chronically can't distinguish between them
have a rather hard time getting by in the world. If I cannot tell the
difference between my image of an open door and the closed door in
front of me, my nose will soon be broken. We learn to tell the difference between our brain's pictures and the reality outside of us. The
image is not the same thing as the actual object, but our brains can be
fooled. And once they are fooled, they will convince the rest of our
bodies that they have the truth. Our bodies naturally trust what our
brains tell them. This is one reason pilots in training for instrument
flight are taught to disregard direct physiological cues and sensations
in their bodies and instead to "trust the instruments." Our bodies
are hardwired to believe physical cues, even when they inaccurately
represent conditions around us.

There are key differences between percepts and images.[33] In the
first place, percepts tend to fade quickly. The picture usually only
stays in place as long as we are looking at it. There is good reason for
that, because if a particular percept stayed in place while we looked
at a new object or while something in the world around us changed,
our brains would be contending with a muddled mess! Images, on
the other hand, can remain vividly in place while all around us is
changing, as long as we continue to attend to them. Second, the content of our percepts is outside the brain; the source of mental images
is internal. Finally, our images are infinitely changeable, whether we
do so intentionally ("What would this room look like in peach?") or
unintentionally, as in dreams or pervasive fears. Percepts in contrast
are constrained by the objects they are representing.

---

33. Kosslyn, *Image and Brain*, 74–75.

Imagination, Dread, and Hope

The imagination serves many purposes. It provides an escape from a painful or boring present. It offers hope for change. But it can also serve to terrify or frighten us. Our imaginations can distract us from the problems of living or help us to resolve them. Our imagination is the grounding of our hope — it is also the seat of our fears. The brain's capacity to envision multiple possibilities is a mixed blessing. We are offered the opportunity to live (at least temporarily) in a world more to our liking, more like it should be. Those large frontal lobes of our brains offer us a platform on which to build a better world. The imagination is the arena in which hope plays out its welcoming invitations.

But the imagination can also plunge us into worlds unsafe for habitation. Instead of quiet beaches or summer meadows, the landscape may offer dark, frightening forests where demons lurk, threatening harm or even death. Danger and risk are as much the coin of the imagination as are safety and comfort. Our evolutionary history likely tuned our brains more to the frequency of fear than to the frequencies of pleasure and peace, as previously discussed, all in a quite effective attempt to preserve our species. So our frightened imaginations may often serve to protect us from real danger and threats to our personal and family safety and to provide us with automatic responses that save life. For that we may be grateful. But at other times the imagination creates its own monsters, and we suffer the same dread that we would if dropped into a lion's den. Our imaginations then are not merely our redemption but also the source of our fear.

We return to our reflections on imagination shortly, but let's turn next to a closer look at its partner in our conversation, the ways in which our brains store and retrieve these many images: the memory.

Chapter 2

WHAT...?
Memory and the Brain

The reality for most survivors who remember toward healing and transformation is that, in the process of working through the memories, they come to an understanding of truth, not as certainty, but as complex and ambiguous knowledge.

—Flora Keshgegian[1]

In the 2001 movie *Memento*, former insurance investigator Leonard Shelby rushes to the aid of his wife who is being assaulted in their home. From a severe blow to the head caused by an accomplice of his wife's assailant, Leonard suffers severe damage to his brain's hippocampus, and when he recovers consciousness, he discovers that he has a resulting *anterograde amnesia*. That is, he can remember details of his life and story quite clearly, up to the time of his injury. What he has lost, however, is the capacity to form *new* memories of anything that has occurred since that blow. New experiences begin to fade immediately and, within ten to fifteen minutes, are gone completely. (This is distinct from the more familiar *retrograde* amnesia in which events prior to the damaging event are no longer available for recall.)

Leonard develops a set of innovative techniques, one of which involves taking Polaroid pictures and recording notes on them immediately, before the significance of those events can fade. He writes

---

1. Flora Keshgegian, *Redeeming Memories: A Theology of Healing and Transformation* (Nashville: Abingdon Press, 2000), 52.

himself notes and has information tattooed on his body. His purpose? To find his wife's killers.

As viewers, we are caught up in the experience of the movie's central character. The film is presented in small bits and chunks of time, opening with the end of the story and proceeding to its beginning. Since at any given time we do not know what has just happened, like Leonard we are without recent memory.

Suddenly Leonard makes a conscious choice to alter the story he is trying to write. When Teddy, the only living person who understands his recent history, confronts him with a painful truth, he changes the written description on Teddy's picture. "Don't believe his lies," he writes, and the die is cast. In that very instant, since we know already how the story turns out, we understand that Leonard has rewritten the entire outcome of this tragic narrative.

The story is an engaging one, not simply because of its intriguing plot and interesting Hollywood take on neuropsychology. It dramatically demonstrates the critical role of memory in the construction of personal identity, and it reminds us of how dependent both memory and story are on the full functioning of that three pounds of nerve tissue that constitute our brains. Further, it raises the important question of how much control we as human beings have over the contents of our memory and whether, in fact, we are as much our memories' victims as we are their creators. Leonard's brain is itself a leading character in his story. We are given a glimpse into the interior world of a neurologically impaired human being and learn about our own brains in the process.

Leonard's alter ego in psychiatric history is a man who is now known by his initials, H.M.[2] This twenty-seven-year-old man suffered severe epileptic seizures, and in 1953 neurosurgeon William Scoville performed surgery that greatly improved his epilepsy but

---

2. Daniel L. Schacter, *Searching for Memory: The Brain, the Mind, and the Past* (New York: Basic Books, 1996), 137–39; John Pinel, *Biopsychology* (Boston: Allyn & Bacon, 1990), 398–406.

damaged the hippocampus and tissue immediately around it, including the amygdala. Under the direction of neuropsychologist Brenda Milner, H.M. became likely the most studied patient in medical history. After the surgery, H.M. maintained significant cognitive skills such as language, perception, and certain types of knowledge, while his IQ actually increased slightly. However, he was unable to remember hospital staff members, including those who had visited him earlier that same day. During testing, he recalled information for up to a period of several minutes, but when asked to identify the same information a little later, he could not even remember having seen these healthcare workers before. He could remember earlier life experiences, but only up until about two or three years before the surgery. H.M.'s tragic experiences nonetheless provided neurology with its first clear opportunities to understand the role of particular brain structures, especially the hippocampus and the medial temporal lobe, in forming and storing memories.

Where Did I Leave Those Keys?

There's surely a reason, as I move into the latter half of my fifties, that I've developed this apparently sudden interest in the workings of the memory. I just can't seem to remember what that reason is. But whatever my current motivation, memory has surely been a central concern for a long time. Not only my memory is at stake here; the memories of those I have tried to help in my work as a pastoral counselor have shaped and motivated my concern.

Memories are the stock-in-trade of psychotherapists and of religious communities alike, to say nothing of what memory means to each of us in our day-to-day living. We remember who we are in the context of both our therapeutic and religious settings, forming our identities as persons and as members of communities larger than ourselves. So as the brain sciences learn more about how the brain remembers, we have available to us new ways to understand and go about this critical business of remembering.

We don't often think about our memories until they begin to fail us. When I can't find my car keys, remember the name of that former student, or recall what I was supposed to pick up at the grocery store, *then* I think about my memory. (Thank goodness for Daytimers and Palm Pilots.) It gets a little more serious for me when I can't recall a story from my own life that might explain why I'm feeling a particular way at a particular time. Many of us have thought even more seriously about the role of memory during a single visit with a person gradually losing memory capacity through the ravages of a process like Alzheimer's disease or someone who has lost memory more quickly following a severe brain injury or stroke. And as many of us age, we find ourselves experiencing what we fear may be a "senior moment." Our unexpressed anxiety is voiced through our humor.

But most of the time, we take our memories for granted. Even when we can't quickly retrieve them, we have this deep conviction that those memories are in there somewhere, if only we can find the right file, or the right key to the file cabinet — or if only we will look hard enough or wait long enough. It is as though they have faded or been misfiled. So we have little systems for recalling them, like the way we remember the number of days in a month by singing a little song to ourselves or make up an acronym to remember items in a grocery list. At other times we hope that, if we get away from the intense work of remembering, the detail will come to us in our rest — perhaps in the middle of the night. But we know those memories are there; we can trust them and they will not go away.

Some of the neuroscientific research has supported our impressions. Many have read about the work of neurosurgeon Wilder Penfield's important work in the 1950s with patients who underwent open brain procedures while they were required to remain conscious.[3] Penfield carefully inserted an electrode into the temporal lobe of

---

3. Schacter, *Searching for Memory*, 77–78; Wilder Penfield, "Consciousness, Memory, and Man's Conditioned Reflexes," in *On the Biology of Learning*, ed. Karl H. Pribram (New York: Harcourt, Brace & World, 1969).

patients and then was able to electrically stimulate the brain while receiving self-reports from patients. These procedures would reportedly elicit vivid images of long-past events — complete with sights, sounds, smells, and touch.

The logical conclusion of these intriguing reports was that nothing we have experienced is ever forgotten. All the events, stories, and images we have collected are resident in the archives of our mind somewhere, no matter how difficult they may be to recall many years later. Given the right set of conditions, or with greatly improved technologies of the brain, we believed those memories could be triggered again and, at least in theory, could be relived as though they were happening the first time — once again with all the richness of our senses. These kinds of reports simply strengthened or confirmed for many of us what we intuitively believed already. The research underscored the vividness and reality of memories we could retrieve.

There is a problem, however. Memory researchers are suggesting now that memories may *not* last forever after all.[4] The optimistic (or sometimes depressing!) sense that we can recall any event under the right circumstances just isn't holding up. Over time, we really *can* forget. That will come as good news to some of us. But there are other memories that we desperately need. One of the problems with Penfield's research was that there was no independent way to verify (or deny) the accuracy of the reported recollections. As convincing as patients' recollections were to them, there was no way to check their reports against data that could support them.

From a strictly pragmatic standpoint, forgetting makes sense. The longer we live, the more experiences our brains must record; the sheer volume of experiences we accumulate increases exponentially the older we grow, crowding the available space. So as time goes by, it is much less likely that we will be able to retrieve particular memories in all their glorious detail. Thankfully, the brain has ways of encod-

---

4. Schacter, *Searching for Memory,* 78.

ing (recording for accurate recall) the really important information so that it will more likely be available when we need it. And there are even steps we can take to strengthen memories. But once again, hold that thought.

What We Mean by "Memory"

Our focus of interest in Leonard's case in *Memento* is *conscious* memory — retrieving those episodes or events that are part of our stories and help us make sense of who we are, where we have come from, and perhaps just as important, where we are headed. That kind of memory concerns us most.

But conscious memories are only part of the picture, since memory includes all those recorded experiences, procedures, and events that have registered somehow in the neural synapses of our brains. Memory too includes at least as many unconscious or implicit memories as it does those of which we are aware.

Memory is also a selective process. The brain cannot record every intricate detail of every event that passes; it must pick and choose. So the brain remembers those events that matter the most at the moment. It also registers only the key details, leaving the rest to be filled in later on by the brain. Listening to adult children recall significant events in conversation with their parents is often revealing. Images of bicycle accidents or family outings that meant much to a child may be long forgotten by a parent who was preoccupied at the time, or vice versa. "I have no memory of that event at all!" is a common response.

Most of those selection processes are automatic; some we cannot override even with real effort. At other times, we can make decisions to remember certain things — and try to forget others. Trying to forget, of course, generally has its opposite effect. If you are not convinced that this can happen, try *not* thinking about a pink elephant for the next five minutes!

How the Brain Remembers

Just exactly how our brains work is still as much mystery as it is known, in spite of all the attention that memory has received in recent decades. There are, after all, by some estimates at least, 100 billion neurons in the human brain.[5] And when we realize that each of those neurons is capable of communicating with dozens of other neurons at any time, the possible number of connections is truly astronomical. So, in spite of all that scientists do know, there is still much more to be discovered. With that caveat, let's proceed.

Memory researchers are approaching the matter from widely divergent directions. Psychologists are studying the mental capacities of memory from a global perspective, identifying types of memory and particular kinds of memory loss. Neuroanatomists are studying the brain structures that support memory or that are damaged in the loss of certain types of memory. Still others are focused on how learning takes place at the level of the individual neuron, or even more specifically what is occurring at the chemical level in synaptic transmission. Each of these approaches is adding its own particular insight to the unfolding understanding of how we remember.

We look first at the types of memory being identified and then at some of the anatomical and neuronal discoveries that are helpful in our understanding. From there we describe some of the characteristics of memory — what lets them fade and what helps them endure, how memories can be distorted and how they can be transformed.

Types of Memory

We need first to acknowledge that memory is not a single, homogeneous capacity of the human brain. It is rather several distinct functions that are related to the general tasks of storing and retrieving information over different lengths of time.

---

5. John J. Ratey, *A User's Guide to the Brain: Perception, Attention, and the Four Theaters of the Brain* (New York: First Vintage Books, 2002), 9.

One of the important distinctions made about memory is the obvious difference between *working memory* — that information that we need for current perceiving and decision-making and behaving — and *long-term memory*. The two different types of memory actually rely on different brain structures.

One rule of thumb about working memory suggests that most human beings can hold seven discrete bits of information in working memory at any one time, give or take two. Perhaps that is the reason our phone numbers are seven digits long, so that the trip from the phone book to the phone need not require constant repetition of those numbers needed to complete that important call. (With the advent of eleven-digit dialing, we will all likely be making more phone calls with the phone book or Palm Pilot in front of us. And thank goodness for speed dialing.)

Working memory has for some time been known to rely particularly on an area called the medial temporal cortex, the layer of cortical tissue that lies "inside" each hemisphere. Even more important, the lateral prefrontal cortex plays a central role in working memory, focusing attention, selecting what the mind will notice, planning, and making decisions.[6] Even the cerebellum, that small ball-shaped structure at the lower back of the brain, participates by coordinating the action of the eyes and body in focusing attention. While a variety of areas of the brain are critical to working memory, the prefrontal lobes fulfill an executive function, directing the activity of the brain and holding key information.

Long-term memory, on the other hand, involves the storage of information for longer than the few seconds or minutes that working memory can hold them. Though the temporal lobe is a critical location for the storage of long-term memories, they are, over time, parceled out to widespread areas in the neocortex, with the special help of the hippocampus, that structure that was damaged in Leonard's encounter with the assailants and in H.M.'s surgery. The

---

6. Joseph LeDoux, *The Emotional Brain: The Mysterious Underpinnings of Emotional Life* (New York: Touchstone, 1996), 274.

pattern to the storage of these memories corresponds, not at all surprisingly, to the areas of the brain that are responsible for carrying out those particular functions in the first place. Visual images, for instance, are stored in the visual (occipital) cortex. Memories for words are located in Broca's and Wernicke's areas in the left temporal cortex. Memories for particular skills are stored in still other areas, including the motor cortex, located immediately in front of the brain's central fissure, or sulcus, which is responsible for initiating movement (see the diagram on p. 31).

The Pathways of Learning

How do memories get from here (short-term memory) to there (long-term memory)? We described in chapter 1 the ways images are formed and register in various locations of the brain. These pathways are responsible for *learning,* the general term applied to the process of recording experiences for later recall. Psychologists call this overall process *encoding,* and the neural pathways that are formed in learning are known as *engrams.* Once the sensory input has been processed in the brain, the hippocampus plays a key role in bringing together various dimensions of the image and then dispensing that information to various locations in the cortex. (This is particularly true for episodic or "story" memories. See below.) Once the story is encoded, or the procedure learned by the rest of the brain, the hippocampus has essentially completed its work and drops out of the picture.[7] This is not a quick back-up of information, however. The process appears to take up to three years to complete.

In the formation of emotional memories, the amygdala is quite active. Here again, once the image has been recorded, the amygdala is less vital and the cortex itself can recall the emotional memory.[8] Some researchers argue that sleep, and particularly dreaming, are critical

7. Joseph LeDoux, *Synaptic Self: How Our Brains Become Who We Are* (New York: Viking, 2002), 251.
8. Ibid.

processes in moving short-term memory into long-term storage, a process known as memory consolidation.[9]

Here the analogy of computers is helpful. Working memory operates a bit like the random access memory (RAM) of our computers that holds the data needed for current calculations. Long-term memory is more like the data stored on the hard drive or floppy drive, data that is accessible by the computer for the times in which it is needed. Like the computer, our brains utilize different brain structures for long-term memory and short-term memory.

A cautionary word about comparing the brain to a computer. While the analogies of hard drives and random access memory may be helpful to describe brain functions, the machine metaphor is a dangerous one. The living brain has profound capacities even the most sophisticated machinery cannot truly duplicate, notwithstanding the amazing progress and potential future of artificial intelligence. Sometimes a metaphor is just a metaphor.

Working memory is not the same as consciousness or awareness. Much of our working memory still operates beneath the surface of our conscious attention, much like the operating system that handles information in our computers. But it does include information the brain needs at the moment, as well as the executive functions needed to manage that information in deciding and problem solving. Working memory by its very definition doesn't stay active for long in the brain. And there are good reasons working memory can't hold on to data too long; it needs to be free to let some data go so it can work on new data.

Long-term memory involves the synaptic recording of experience at separate but precise locations in the brain. Working memory and long-term memory are in constant dialogue. Working memory relies on the data it can retrieve from long-term memory to recognize and identify objects in the environment, as we described in chapter 1. The brain recalls the data as it needs it and, as we see in the next section,

9. Ibid., 10; James Ashbrook and Carol Rausch Albright, *The Humanizing Brain: Where Religion and Neuroscience Meet* (Cleveland: Pilgrim Press, 1997), 95–98.

the brain uses that data in ways that meet its needs at the moment. At the same time, the brain is gradually moving information from short-term memory into long-term memory.

We rely on still other dimensions of memory. *Semantic memory* refers to the knowledge of concepts and facts, regardless of whether we have directly experienced them and whether we can recall any personal stories associated with learning them. Psychologists generally include broad information about the world in this category. *Procedural memory* involves the development of skills and habits, such as playing the piano or reciting multiplication tables or the Lord's Prayer. *Autobiographical memory,* or what psychologist Endel Tulving called *episodic memory,* describes the recall of explicit personal incidents that help shape our lives.[10] This type of memory is particularly important to us in our understanding of the role of the brain in storytelling in chapter 3. As we see later, some forms of memory can remain intact, even when others are lost. H.M., for instance, learned to track a moving target even though he couldn't recall ever having done so before.[11]

Whether these different types of memory require different brain structures to do their work (and they most likely do), they surely suggest to us that memory is a many-faceted concept. What makes the picture even more intriguing is the realization that the brain appears to store none of these memories as "packages" in single locations. As we noted briefly, despite our experience that memories come from a single location in our brains, neuroscientists contend that different dimensions of each of those memories are stored in separate locations in the brain.[12] Diverse sections all over the brain contribute information to the recall of any one image, event, or story. Visual details, sounds, smells, and touch dimensions of a particular memory, for instance,

---

10. Schacter, *Searching for Memory,* 17.

11. Ibid., 164; Pinel, *Biopsychology,* 402.

12. See, e.g., Antonio Damasio, *Descartes' Error: Emotion, Reason, and the Human Brain* (New York: G. P. Putnam's Sons, 1994), 84.

are each stored in their own locations in the brain and pulled together to reconstruct a representation of the event. The hippocampus, that region entrusted with coordinating the storage of long-term memories, appears also to reunite those separate dimensions of memory during recall and create their sense of coherence.

The emotional responses we connect with certain events are housed in still other areas of the brain, primarily within the limbic system and in the frontal lobes. Most of our memories pass through this limbic system where they were "tagged" with the feelings we had in response to those events when we first experienced them. Sometimes our emotional memories emerge even when we have no recollection of the events that first prompted them. So a hymn might trigger a sudden feeling of sadness, for instance, though its connection with the funeral of a friend from long ago may have been lost. How the brain pulls all these memory parts back together into one coherent — and usually accurate — memory is still something of a mystery, referred to as the "binding problem" (see discussion in chapter 1). A number of theories have been proposed for this system, and one of the more intriguing is the recent discovery that the brain may actually generate new neuronal tissue throughout adulthood. Until very recently, neuroscientists had believed that the central nervous system (at least the neocortex) was about the only system in the human body that did *not* replace damaged or deteriorating cells. But new data suggest that brains may actually generate new nerve tissue.[13] As to how the brain pulls the right pieces of memory together at the right time, researchers speculate that new neurons may be generated at the instant an event is recorded, and therefore have identical "birthdays." When the brain recalls those events, it would pull together information from neurons generated at the same time, resulting in a coherent memory. While intriguing, this theory has yet to gain wide acceptance in the field.

---

13. Elizabeth Gould, Alison J. Reeves, Michael S. A. Graziano, and Charles Gross, "Neurogenesis in the Neocortex of Adult Primates," *Science* 286 (October 15, 1999): 548–52.

So what do we know about the mechanics of memory? How does the brain actually record these experiences? We first offer a brief introduction to the ways our nerve cells work and then a word about the neurochemistry of memory.

You've Got Some Nerve

What neuroscientists generally agree about is the critical way in which learning and memory rely on changes in the synapses or connections between nerve cells for their communication. So a word about how neurons work.[14]

Some neurons communicate directly with muscles or glands in the body. When I want to move my arm, for instance, a signal is sent to the muscles where it triggers the contraction that will move that arm. The signal begins in the frontal cortex as an intention, which then signals the motor strip in the cortex. From there the signal crosses several synapses before my arm moves. But how does this help explain memory?

Neurons in the brain and in the central nervous system, and in the whole body for that matter, communicate primarily by way of electric-like impulses that travel down the long extension of the cell body known as the axon (see the diagram on p. 63). This impulse is known as an *action potential,* referring to the ways electrical charges change within the cell and travel down the axon. At the end of that axon is an array of spikes referred to as an axon terminal containing many "buttons." Each of these buttons holds tiny packets of a specific chemical known as a neurotransmitter. When an impulse (or action potential) reaches the end of the terminal, it prompts the release of a burst of neurotransmitter into the tiny space (the synapse) between that cell and the tiny treelike appendages, known as dendrites, on

---

14. This discussion is by necessity simplified; anyone wanting more in-depth discussion of these complex processes should consult any good introduction to neurobiology, or see LeDoux, *Synaptic Self,* for an excellent chapter on these processes.

Neuron

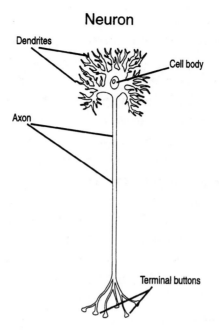

the next cell. This burst of chemicals is taken up into the dendritic spines of the second cell (referred to as the postsynaptic cell), where it induces an electrical change. If it produces a strong enough change, an impulse or action potential begins again. From there it will find its way down the axon of the second cell. (There are some neurons that communicate by direct mechanical contact with other neurons, but their function lies beyond the scope of this volume.)

For decades, scientists have understood that learning and memory are the result of strengthening synaptic connections between neurons. That is, some chemical or physical change in the two cells that are communicating with each other occurs so that firing the first neuron is more likely to fire the second the next time around. What scientists are uncovering is a more precise description of the mechanics (and "chemics") of those processes.[15]

---

15. Ibid., particularly chapters 3–6; Pinel, *Biopsychology*, 448–51.

Most of the time, once a cell has fired, it returns to rest, having done its job. But when learning has occurred, changes have also taken place in the synapses and in the structures on either side of that synapse. The receiving cell has changed so that it is ready and tuned to the preceding cell. So learning a new piano piece requires intense effort, because more energy is required to fire across the synapses to unprepared receptors. With practice, however, those receptors are "tuned" and ready to fire more easily. This process has induced a new, longer-lasting level of electrical responsiveness in the second cell known as long-term potentiation, or LTP. Postsynaptic cells apparently have ways to recognize the specific cells that trigger the responses — that is, to "remember" them — so they won't fire in response to just any old cell. The presynaptic cell may also be changed in learning.[16] A second way that these connections are reinforced is that the postsynaptic cell may be induced to produce additional dendrites, again increasing the number of synaptic connections and the likelihood of firing when fired upon by that particular neuron.

This LTP can be induced in several ways. Frequent rapid firing of the axon may induce the change ("practice makes perfect"). Adding up the charges of two adjacent cells may reach a level of excitation in the second cell to link them (two things happen at once and the neuron says, "these must belong together"). Chemical and direct electrical charges can also induce these changes.

There is, of course, a huge gap between comprehending such technical processes as long-term potentials and synaptic transmission and understanding how the brain forms memories of important life stories. Understanding the neurochemical processes between two cells does little to instruct our practices of ministry. This gap in understanding between what science does know and what it does not is important to acknowledge. For our purposes, it is equally important to understand that learning and memory take place in bodies,

16. LeDoux, *Synaptic Self,* 141.

that they are grounded in biological life processes, and that they are incredibly sophisticated. Neuroscientists are tackling these issues, currently at levels that concern simple learning responses, but in the process they are building a portfolio of procedures and knowledge that will eventually help us describe the biological mechanics of the critical human processes of thinking and feeling.

So What Does It All Mean for Us?

A central implication of all this research is that the brain actually reconstructs our memories each time we recall them.[17] There's a reason we call it re-membering. As a result, we never re-member any event in exactly the same way twice. In another sense, we never re-member the same object or event twice. Instead, we are re-creating or re-imagining that event each time we recall it. What a disconcerting thought! Those memories that we trust for our daily activities are regularly being rebuilt as we go along. They seem so real — and yet they are the result of millions of neurons firing to bring together again multiple pieces of a puzzle. What a blow to our certainty about our memories! There is a reason that Harvard psychologist Daniel Schacter refers to memory's "fragile power."[18]

As we have said before, memory is not a single, simple function of the brain. It is multifaceted and supported by distinctive structures. We have already noted that procedural memory is different from semantic or episodic memory and that brain damage or illness resulting in loss of one kind of memory may retain other memory capacities. It is not at all uncommon for persons with deficits in one area of memory to have other types of memory fully intact. It is common in worship services in retirement communities, for instance, to observe Alzheimer's patients who, though they are unable to recall what they ate for breakfast that morning, can recite the Lord's Prayer or sing a

---

17. Antonio Damasio, reported in Schacter, *Searching for Memory,* 66.
18. Schacter, *Searching for Memory,* 133.

familiar hymn without missing a beat. And persons unable to recall the word for a shovel might nevertheless be able to demonstrate its use by picking it up and digging in the ground.

Further, these memory systems operate at different rates of speed. We noted in chapter 1 for instance, that a threatening object can trigger an emotional response well before our conscious mind is even aware of the presence of the threatening object. Likewise, emotional memories can erupt well before we can recall the emotional event that prompted the feeling in the first place — or even when we are unable to remember it at all. Emotional memories are much more difficult to change than are our memories of events or of facts, which is undoubtedly one of the reasons they seem so irrational to us long after we've realized the event is over and the threat no longer exists.[19] Repeated comments from others or from ourselves that "It's all right now" often do little to relieve the anxiety that results from an emotional memory. In part, this is a consequence of the fact that many more neurons connect the amygdala to the cortex than go in the opposite direction. That is, emotionally charged memories have more supporting circuits and flow more readily to influence thoughts than thoughts do to influence feelings.

Let's remind ourselves at this point, like we did with our reflections on image and imagination, that for the most part our memories are trustworthy. Given that we rely on them for our very survival, they must work rather well. What we are lifting up here is the need for some humility about memory's power. We live as though they are true — and yet the very complexity of the processes of remembering highlights memory's potential risks.

One conclusion many scientists have drawn from these multiple limitations to memory is that the brain in fact has evolved for purposes very different from the detailed, photographic recording of particular events. What cognitive scientists in particular are asking concerns the realistic purpose of memory. What is memory really

---

19. LeDoux, *The Emotional Brain*, 203.

for? Most often the answer given is survival or sex, or even more often, both. That is, our brains have evolved primarily to protect our bodies from potential harm and to increase our likelihood of reproduction. Psychologist Michael Gazzaniga makes it even simpler: "the evolutionary perspective on memory is that its main function is to localize things in space. Where did I hide the food? Where is my cache? Where is the base camp I just wandered away from to find food?"[20] So it's quite important that we be able to remember objects in the environment with which we've had frightening experiences in the past. It's almost as important, but not quite, to be able to remember persons with whom we can have affectionate, nurturing relationships to improve the likelihood that our species will continue.

Memory seldom seems capable of meeting the high demands of accuracy and completeness that we demand of it. It's not quite the same brain trying to recall an event as the one that recorded it in the first place. And yet we often continue to experience our memories as though they were digital photographs and recordings that *ought* to be available to us on demand. We need to be able to distinguish between what the brain is good at and what it doesn't do so well.

Worship and pastoral counseling both operate on the foundation of memory. From the common instructions to "remember your baptism" and "as often as you do this, do it in remembrance of me," we recognize that memory is not automatic. By observing that memories may be less intentionally triggered by symbols of water, fire, light, or a cross, we grasp the common truth that some memories come unbidden. Why does memory work that way? What are our brains doing that makes that all possible? With questions like these "in mind," let's look at some of the ways that memory can fail, because several of these are critical to our understanding of worship and pastoral care.

---

20. Michael Gazzaniga, *The Mind's Past* (Berkeley: University of California Press, 1998), 39.

Risks

There are at least five troubling ways our memories make us aware of themselves: lost memories, partial memories, painful memories, distorted memories, and false memories.

Lost memories. If I forget my car keys, I have a loss of memory — unfortunately this is not an uncommon occurrence in my case. It's a more serious problem if I forget where I live. Even more tragically, some persons forget who they are — they no longer remember their names, their families, or their histories. We get used to the little memory losses we all experience. It is infinitely harder to adjust to a total loss of memory, either in our own minds or the minds of those persons close to us. Who we are depends on what we can remember.

Of course, only at its most extreme, through stroke, injury, or a degenerative disease like Alzheimer's, can all memory — at least conscious memory — appear to be lost. Sometimes particular memories are lost while the rest of a person's autobiographical (episodic) memory appears to be complete and remain intact. Sigmund Freud's emphasis on unconscious process, of course, was built on notions of suppression and repression of memories, those that were too painful or too directly in violation of consciously held values. They just don't fit, they are not acceptable, and so they are not remembered. While memory researchers and brain scientists are less enamored of such notions, the conviction is held so deeply in our culture — and in our religious and psychotherapeutic communities — that it is hard to think of memory without thinking about repressed memories. Some of the dilemmas associated with that conviction are discussed in more depth below when we look at false memories. But the concept does lead later to our consideration of memories that hurt.

Remember that memory researchers are suggesting that memories don't necessarily last forever.[21] Some loss of memories is really quite adaptive for the "full" brain, which otherwise would struggle like

---

21. Daniel L. Schacter, ed., *Memory Distortion: How Minds, Brains, and Societies Reconstruct the Past* (Cambridge, Mass.: Harvard University Press, 1995), 77–81.

the proverbial full hard drive on a computer that can no longer accept any more information and takes forever sorting through the data it already has. I still remember the phone number of my childhood home. It does me little good some fifty years later, and fortunately seldom comes to mind when I want to call my current home. But remembering my home number, along with two office numbers and a cell phone, suggests that if I were able to forget that ancient number, perhaps there would be more room to store the number of my plumber or the pizza shop for more ready recall. Fortunately there is much unnecessary data that my brain has forgotten.

Partial memories. Our brains are selective by necessity. There is no way, and usually no need, to remember all details of all events, Dr. Penfield's conclusions notwithstanding. The brain decides what is important to recall based on its needs at that time. Witnesses to a bank robbery, for instance, will register in exquisite detail a gun that is pointed in their direction and barely notice the face or clothing of the robber. When it comes time to identify suspects in a lineup, their brains need the information that was less vital at the time and not nearly so vividly recorded. So it's not surprising, if sometimes inconvenient, that there are gaps in even the most emotionally charged memories.

When a detail is lacking, the brain automatically fills in the blanks so that it has a complete story or image. Again, what may look like a design flaw is actually an advantage, because our brains would become clogged very quickly after only a few short years of living if it had to find space for all that intricate detail. Or the brain would take so long sorting through all the episodes and details that the need for the information would have long passed before we retrieved it! So the brain compresses the information, selecting particularly important details to represent the whole event, or choosing one image to stand in for the others and forgetting the rest.

So in a real sense, all memories are partial, no matter how vivid they appear during recall. But we tend to experience partial memories as troublesome in two different kinds of circumstances: when we desperately need that missing bit of information to complete a story, argument, or defense, or when we discover that our brains have filled in the blanks with information that didn't really belong there in the first place.

Painful memories. Some memories are troublesome not because they are missing, but because they won't go away. Memories of traumatic experiences, like sexual or physical abuse or violence encountered on a dark street or during a war, can last for many years following the event. They often intrude on the thoughts and feelings of survivors while they are wide awake and can disrupt sleep, leading to exhaustion. Common sights or sounds associated with the traumatic event, such as the closing of a door, thunder, or the backfiring of a car, can trigger such recurring memories. Feelings of anxiety to the point of terror can also erupt without apparent prompting.

Called "shell shock" by psychologists treating World War I soldiers, such intrusive and painful memories have become part of the syndrome now known as post-traumatic stress disorder (PTSD). The range of events that can produce the symptoms has been extended to include any circumstances that involve real or perceived severe danger or threat to life. Unwanted, unpredictable, and intrusive memories are the most notable features of the disorder, along with attention difficulties and the avoidance of reminders of the traumatizing event.[22]

Similar (if milder) forms of intrusive memories can afflict any of us whose symptoms fall short of a diagnosis of full-blown PTSD. Hurtful, unbidden memories can emerge during a conversation with a partner or friend, during worship or a movie, or even while dreaming. Though such experiences may be less frequent and disruptive than post-traumatic memories, they can be unsettling and distracting as if they are calling for our immediate and careful attention.

Some traumatic memories are prompted by events of broad social significance. Until the terrorist attacks of September 11, 2001,

---

22. American Psychiatric Association, *Diagnostic and Statistical Manual of Mental Disorders,* 4th ed. (Washington, D.C., American Psychiatric Association, 1994), 424–29.

the most familiar national event people were able to recall was the assassination of John F. Kennedy in November 1963. The famous question, "Do you remember where you were when you first heard about Kennedy's shooting?" still draws detailed answers from most people who were at least five years of age at the time. Psychologists studying this phenomenon developed the term "flashbulb memory" to describe the sense of vivid clarity and detail that characterized these memories, and the conviction that people felt about the accuracy of those recollections.

Evidence has accumulated suggesting that memories formed during times of emotional trauma may well be better remembered and last longer than memories of routine events. The more emotionally engaging the event (either positively or negatively), the more accurately it will be remembered.

Even these memories can suffer distortions and decay, though both are usually less likely in memories of emotionally charged events than they are for memories of more routine events. The dimension of the memory most likely to persist is the central meaning of the event, its "gist," while particular details may change with the passage of time.[23]

Distorted memories. Memories are subject to distortion from many sources, including misinformation, mood, neurobiological and psychological processes including trauma, and extinction or forgetting.[24] Our brains (especially the right hemisphere for most persons) are designed to think in terms of wholes, as we noted in chapter 1. So the process of filling out incomplete memories is a normal, regular dimension of the way the brain functions all the time, and most of the time it works just fine. The filled-in details help give the story we are recalling coherence and "glue," and most often, the new details support the importance or significance of the memory. But on some occasions, those apparently minor details turn out to hold an importance that they never had before.

---

23. Schacter, *Searching for Memory*, 209.
24. Schacter, *Memory Distortion*.

The brain uses several different sources for filling in the gaps, generally influenced by what the individual needs at the moment. Often the brain calls on what it generally knows about the object or type of event being remembered for missing details. Without even being aware of it, the brain may be presented with subliminal cues ahead of time (intentionally or unintentionally) and so is prompted to recall a certain type of detail — a phenomenon known as "priming." Counseling several couples with marital conflict will likely prime my brain for words like "love," "disappointment," or "affection." I'm more likely to use words about relationship when I return home, or even stop on the way to pick up flowers! The brain also draws on the past and selects details that make present experiences either consistent with or different from the past, depending on the individual's current needs. The brain can surreptitiously select details that support either a sense of specialness or of unworthiness, as in the case of depression. The brain recalls details that are consistent with its current mood.

False memories. One of the most highly charged areas of life in which memory's reliability has been called into question is the now infamous *repressed memory syndrome,* particularly among victims of childhood sexual and physical abuse. It's been a painful story in itself, weaving together the traumatic realities of abuse with what we are learning about the ways the mind works.

Many of us have ministered to or known persons who have had traumatic experiences of physical or sexual abuse decades earlier in their lives. Most often it's been a family member or close friend who perpetrated the abuse. Less often it's been someone totally unknown to the victim. Often they are memories the victim has recalled, but has never had a safe place to tell. A number of women (and fewer men) who previously had no conscious memories of such events would recover them, usually in the context of psychotherapy, which they sought for some other reason, such as depression, thought disturbances, or unexplained anxiety around other people. These memories would occur spontaneously as victims attempted to fill in gaps in their remembered histories. At other times, these memories surfaced with the help of a therapist who suggested that their symptoms indicated a history of abuse. Some of these victims made public their accusations of their abusers. Some took legal action and won sizable settlements in courts. Justice was demanded on behalf of these young victims.

About a decade ago these stories received national attention. In a number of highly publicized cases, the alleged victims of remembered abuse later recanted their stories and sought to reconcile with their families. Too often, these families remained torn apart and unable to overcome the painful history of false accusations. A backlash then developed from family members and other accused perpetrators of these horrendous crimes against vulnerable victims. Even some assumed victims have turned to accuse their therapists of misleading them. Some overzealous therapists have been disciplined for insisting on the presence and truth of these "memories," even when clients have resisted their likelihood.[25]

One unfortunate outcome of these highly visible cases is that some true victims of childhood sexual or physical abuse have been forced to doubt the reality of their memories. Some therapists have been reluctant to follow up on the possibility of such memories for fear of lawsuits or licensing discipline if those memories are ultimately unsupportable. Still other victims have continued to believe their memories but have been stopped from confronting the alleged perpetrators given the possibility of lawsuits and deep family conflict.

It is tragic that real perpetrators of sexual violence against children now have ammunition to support their inevitable denial and real victims may be silenced by this turn of events — not to mention its coverage by the press. Justice has likely been denied in many cases of real abuse on the basis of our current confusion about how to evaluate or confirm these memories and the accusations that follow. It is also sad, of course, that some victims may have been deceived by themselves and their therapists, and that whole families have suffered.

25. Joseph de Rivera and Theodore Sarbin, *Believed-In Imaginings: The Narrative Construction of Reality* (Washington, D.C.: American Psychological Association, 1998).

Because autobiographical memories are not simple storage of passively experienced events, but are rather interpretive reconstructions, we must treat the external validity of memories with a high degree of caution. "The waters of memory recovery are treacherous and should be walked through very carefully."[26] This notion presents a critical dilemma given that our personal and communal identities depend on those very memories to the point that some consider memory to constitute the soul itself. This paradox, which has faced psychotherapists, pastors, and lawyers for decades, appears to be a paradox we must live with, respecting both the validity of our memories and at the same time holding them up to the light of suspicion.

All this turmoil leads us to ask important questions, though, about the role of memory in our lives. At times it seems that people are capable of believing almost anything — things that boggle our minds — and they can believe them with as much conviction as we have about the reality of our families, of our houses, or of our God. What does it tell us about ourselves that we need so desperately to believe what we remember? These questions surface again in chapter 3 when we explore the role of story and identity. But in the meantime we'll consider more carefully the act of remembering.

The Re-Membered Self

The very act of recalling a life event — re-membering — requires drawing back together those dimensions of experience that have been dissected from each other and stored in multiple distant vaults in the brain. The pieces must all fit together if we are to have a convincing, coherent picture of our histories that can support the experience of personal identity and direction that life requires. The pieces of our memories are scattered in patterns across the billions of synapses throughout the brain, and reconstructing a memory demands that

---

26. LeDoux, *The Emotional Brain*, 245.

the brain locate and bind together again the multiple discrete dimensions of experience. The brain accomplishes this incomprehensible task thousands of times a day.

As we noted earlier, each time a memory is reconstructed, it is a new memory. Regardless of its similarity to earlier recollections, the new memory varies at least in some small detail from the memories of the same event we recalled before. Because memories constitute the self, each time we remember an event from our own lives, the self is transformed. The act of re-membering is an act of self-reconstruction. Each time we re-member the events that have shaped our lives, we are re-membering who we are.

Such reconstruction of the self sounds both simple and risky. Or even worse, it raises the specter of unrestricted change—like a runaway train. Yet the brain is also a conservative organ, protecting its maps of the world and of the self that it has laboriously constructed over years or decades of time. The pattern of reconstruction is generally as slow and deliberate as road construction crews during a Chicago summer. It is no wonder that persons wanting to change the very core of themselves wish desperately for a moment or a word to make it all happen, rather than the time-consuming process that it invariably requires. Memory reconstruction is a gradual and deliberate process.

Memory, Imagination, and the Soul

Most of us rightly understand the central significance of memory in structuring a dependable sense of self. Without memories, at least without explicit autobiographical memories, we suspect that there is no sense of personal being, of existing in any continuity of space and time. And there is indeed a decreasing capacity to relate to other persons, a central dimension of our experience of being human.[27] The

27. Warren Brown, Nancey Murphy, and H. Newton Malony, eds., *Whatever Happened to the Soul? Scientific and Theological Portraits of Human Nature* (Minneapolis: Fortress Press, 1998), 101–3.

unavoidable implication is that, as memories are lost or die, the self becomes lost or dies also, as does the soul. "We are our memories, and without them, we are nothing."[28] "Without working memory, nothing is personally meaningful. A person has no unique identity and no sense of continuity, since the person cannot connect his or her present with the past. In truth, the person loses his or her soul...."[29]

Memories serve to locate us in time, providing us with a sense of past, present, and future. Without memories we are incapable of experiencing a sense of self. Lacking memories, we are even less capable of experiencing the transcendent dimensions of self expressed by the word "soul." Even apart from its intimations of immortality, the notion of soul captures a sense of the sacredness of the self and suggests relationship with the divine. Soul communicates a sense of both transcendent timelessness and embodied timeliness, of unity with the Other and unique personhood.

Soul also suggests a sense of direction or of heading somewhere. Memories are critical to our sense of movement and purpose in life. Because we know we have a past we anticipate a future. What we learn from that past gives us glimpses of what might yet come to be. Memories are the road signs for our experience of journey. As we noted in chapter 1, imagination and memory interact in our experiences of the present. Here we can go even further and acknowledge that much of the content of the imagination (and of an imagined future) comes from the store of memories encoded in the synapses of the brain. We draw from those memories a map of the course of life, and with the help of our imaginations, we project that course out into the future.

The word used to describe the path of an object hurtling through space is *trajectory*. When scientists know the speed, location, and forces acting on the object (such as wind resistance and gravity), they are able to calculate with some precision where that object will be in the next hour, week, or year. In fact, our brains are making similar

---

28. LeDoux, *Synaptic Self*, 97.
29. Ashbrook and Albright, *The Humanizing Brain*, 173.

calculations when we throw or catch a ball, anticipate traffic at a four-way stop, or reach for the outstretched hand of a friend who is walking toward us. In working memory, we are able to record where the object or person of interest has been, what direction it is moving, and when it will reach a point at which we will either make contact or avoid a collision! From nanosecond to nanosecond the brain is calling on memory of recent movements and anticipating the next.

Certainly the processes by which the brain calls on long-term memory to anticipate future life events are much less precise and dependable. Whether we intentionally plan for the future or our brains construct scenarios of which we are not consciously aware, many events or forces can interfere with the future course the brain maps out for itself. Nevertheless, it does not stretch plausibility far to suggest that the brain is regularly and automatically consulting memories of past events to provide at least tentative pictures of what is yet to come.

We revisit the notion of trajectory in chapters 3 and 5. For our purposes now, let us suggest that *soul* be understood as *a process (rather than a static entity) grounded in both memory and imagination, in fact operating at the intersection of remembered history and anticipated future. Soul paradoxically embodies both the unique dimensions of personhood lived out within the boundaries of body and time and unboundaried connection with the rest of creation.* Our brains are not the isolated, individual organs they at first appear to be. The human brain is above all a social brain, actively seeking connection with others.

Memory and the Social Brain

We noted earlier that the human brain has evolved capacities for relationship with other human beings unseen in any other species. Not only do we have capacity for relationships; we cannot live without them. Because we have traded a rich repertoire of fixed instincts for the ability to adapt to a wide array of environments, human beings require extensive nurturing during childhood and intensive mentoring and training. And beyond the practicalities of living, the need for nurture and affection is built into our nervous systems. Children left alone die.

Even the neurons that make up the brain are social by nature. Shortly after conception the fetus begins producing primitive nerve cells at the rate of 250,000 per minute![30] These nerve cells travel to various locations in the developing brain and then form the axons and dendrites that allow them to communicate with their neighbors. Those that make connections survive. Those that don't undergo cell death. "From the beginning of its being built, the brain is a social brain, the neurons making connections with their neighbors or dying for lack of contact." From a total of 200 billion neurons in the brain during the later stages of pregnancy, only half will survive and become part of the infant's brain.[31]

Many capacities of the human brain further underscore its social nature. Capacities for language, for empathy, for face recognition, and for emotional expression and regulation provide structural evidence that the brain is built for relationship with other human beings. Difficulties in any of these capacities severely limit our abilities to interact and bond with each other.

Autobiographical memories, by their very nature, would appear to be individual and private matters. We own our memories and understand that they are not easily transferred from one person to another. Yet our capacity for recall and for language, let alone that impulse that we all experience to share memories, suggests that memories are also at the center of our capacities to relate to each other. Memories shared with another are relived and re-created each time they are given voice. For human beings to have memories is not enough; we also must share them. For us to remember is not enough; we also want to be remembered.

---

30. Ratey, *A User's Guide to the Brain*, 23–26.
31. Ibid., 23.

Such a status for memories has important implications for spiritual practice, as chapters 5 and 6 show. For the time being, let us briefly note the liabilities in thinking of memory as "owned" solely by one person. While autobiographical memories are in one sense personal and private, memories also structure communities — relationships, families, communities of faith, ethnic groups, and nations. In a real sense, our communities at all levels are defined by their remembered stories just as individual human beings are.

We know that families help carry the stories of each other, as evidenced by the ways young children hungrily devour stories of their own births and early lives, the ways families gathered together around the Thanksgiving table tell stories and keep them alive for each other and for generations of children who were not present for the original events. So memories are also held of each other, and to that extent, our selves, and our souls, are also entrusted to those communities of which we are a part.

Pastoral theologian John Patton has argued for the centrality of memory as a quality of God to which we give expression in our caring relationships with each other. "God created human beings for relationship with God and with one another. God continues in relationship with creation by hearing us, remembering us, and bringing us into relationship with one another. Human care and community are possible because of our being held in God's memory; therefore, as members of caring communities we express our caring analogically with the caring of God by also hearing and remembering."[32]

Such a declaration is both a hopeful and a tragic one. As we live in vital communities that listen to the stories each member has to tell, we are reminded that our stories are also being heard, and remembered, by a "great cloud of witnesses." The sharing of more intimate memories with trusted others — a spouse, a pastor, a spiritual director, a counselor — are ways of adding breadth to the life of our memories.

---

32. John Patton, *Pastoral Care in Context: An Introduction to Pastoral Care* (Louisville: Westminster John Knox Press, 1993), 6.

The tragedy is that we so often shy away from those who suffer losses of memory. We are made uncomfortable when a person dear to us becomes unable to recall our last visit or even recognize us. Or we are made aware of the fragility of our own bodies, of our own memories. Just when persons are most in need of others to serve as memory carriers for them, they are abandoned. What a difference it makes to persons in the early stages of a deteriorating memory to anticipate that others will remember them, that their stories will not be forgotten. In that context we turn to the role of stories — those narratives that bind our memories, and our imaginations, into wholes.

Chapter 3

IF ONLY...
Stories Human and Divine

If you want to know me, then you must know my story, for my story defines who I am. And if I want to know myself, to gain insight into the meaning of my own life, then I, too, must come to know my own story. —Dan McAdams[1]

Memory and imagination, the subjects of the first two chapters, are bound together in stories. We understand and shape who we are through the stories we tell about our own lives. Because we are human beings, we tell stories. And just as truly we listen to stories. Family identity too is shaped by the stories we remember and tell about our generations. We express our faith in the stories we remember and tell about God and the people of God. When human and divine stories intersect, new images of the world emerge. So a key question for our current exploration is, how can pastoral care and worship help persons and families weave their personal stories with God's story?

Stories are at the heart of ministry, whether they are told or heard in the sanctuary, the hospital room, the prison, or the counseling office. Storytelling is at the very heart of being human and of caring for other human beings. Much has been written about the role of story in pastoral care and counseling, and certainly in worship, over the last several years with the maturing of narrative methods in many disciplines, including preaching, psychology, theology, and pastoral care.

---

1. Dan McAdams, *Stories We Live By: Personal Myths and the Making of the Self* (New York: William Morrow, 1993), 11.

In chapter 3 we look first at the brain as storyteller. Then we next take a brief look at what some pastoral theologians have been saying about story and explore some of the ways stories function in personal, family, and community identities. Finally we explore some of the implications those discussions have for caring and worshiping.

Stories and the Brain

Storytelling is a universal human activity. Persons in all cultures of the world tell stories. Like perceptions, images, and memories, stories are also products of our brains. They require each other. Our brains automatically put images and memories together into stories in the brain's ongoing automatic processes of making sense of experience and of the world.

Storytelling depends on our human capacity for language, which is a capacity that only the human species has, at least to the degree we do. With extensive training and just the right context, some other primates can be taught a very limited language. But none come close either to the complexity of human symbolic language or the ease with which we learn to speak.[2] Some evolutionary theorists argue that language is instinctual, while others see language as the by-product of capacities developed for other purposes, such as group cohesiveness and survival.

We humans have a proportionately large neocortex compared to other species and (in particular) large frontal lobes which carry out the work of attention, working memory, and planning. We therefore have incomparable capacities for images, symbols, and language. We have already seen how these differences can free us from bondage to the present and the way things are. We are capable of symbolically imagining the world in different ways, of painting pictures of the ways the world could be. That capacity is at once both our strength and

---

2. Terrence W. Deacon, *The Symbolic Species: The Co-Evolution of Language and the Brain* (New York: W. W. Norton, 1997), 42.

our vulnerability, and those capacities are grounded in the structures and operations of the brain.

Two Brains or One?

At long last we need to say something about the difference between the right brain and the left brain. The "split-brain" research of psychobiologist Roger Sperry and associates during the 1970s, which uncovered the remarkably different skills of the two hemispheres of the neocortex, hit virtually every newsstand, bookstore, and broadcast medium with varying degrees of accuracy. You may remember that during that time, surgeons treated a number of patients for severe epilepsy, which commonly starts in one hemisphere and travels across the corpus callosum to the other, by severing the connection between the hemispheres, but only as a last resort to stop the spread of seizures. The surgeries were often quite effective, and after surgery these patients appeared quite normal in everyday encounters. Yet careful studies of those patients revealed how the two hemispheres of the brain carry out rather different tasks and can function in some strange ways when they are not allowed to communicate with each other.

Psychologist Robert Ornstein, one of the early researchers in the field, turned away from his study of the asymmetry of the brain when he saw the sometimes absurd applications that were being touted. He now calls those early misuses of that groundbreaking research "dichotomania."[3] While some neuroscientists continue to seek the particular locations of different brain functions, more recent research has focused on the workings of the whole brain and on systems of brain structures working together. Neuroscientists are concluding that complex systems of neurons are responsible for our most critical human capacities rather than locating responsibility for any important capacity solely in one area of the brain. Some areas make

---

3. Robert Ornstein, *The Right Mind* (New York: Harcourt Brace, 1997), 87–96.

key contributions, so damage to those areas results in loss of a particular function. But awareness that the whole brain is necessary for our living, thinking, and feeling has become increasingly evident.

That being said, it is still widely understood that the left side of our brains is a little bit better than the other side at particular tasks, and vice versa. When one side is even a little better than the other at a given task, over time it assumes primary responsibility for the things it does well. And as we shall see, both sides of the brain are critical to our tasks of making sense of the world. Without exaggerating the differences, let's say a word about the brain and story.

Plot and Context

The two hemispheres of our brain communicate constantly with each other and in healthy individuals function as a whole rather than as two separate "brains." As previously noted, this communication is accomplished primarily through that bundle of neurons known as the corpus callosum, though hormonal and other neuronal connections help ensure good communication in both directions. Yet each side contributes uniquely to our storytelling. At the risk of giving away the punch line and severely oversimplifying the process, the brain's left hemisphere grinds out the plots of our stories, while the right hemisphere provides the context. The left is the writer, and the right hemisphere is the editor — or something like that. Let's look at those differences more closely.

Dartmouth psychologist Michael Gazzaniga has described a system in the left hemisphere that he has dubbed the "interpreter."[4] This system is designed (or has evolved) to write stories about what is happening in the world and does so even when it is not receiving appropriate sensory input. Gazzaniga conducted studies with split-brain patients in which he placed one picture in the right field of vision so that only the left hemisphere could "see" it, and another in the left

---

4. Michael Gazzaniga, *The Mind's Past* (Berkeley: University of California Press, 1998), 23–27.

field of vision for the right hemisphere. A picture of a chicken claw was shown to the left hemisphere (which controls the right hand) and a snow scene to the right (which controls the left hand). The patient was then shown pictures that included a chicken and a shovel and asked to select the ones that matched what the patient had just seen. One patient chose the chicken with his right hand and the shovel with his left. When asked to explain what had happened, he proclaimed that he could use the shovel to clean out a chicken coop. According to Gazzaniga, the left hemisphere (which is responsible for language — the right hemisphere is essentially mute) automatically constructed a story that made sense of the patient's unconscious actions without benefit of the information contained in the right hemisphere. In effect, the patient watched himself do something he did not understand, so he made up a story.

The left brain by its very nature constructs stories to make sense of what's happening in the world. The brain writes stories to explain otherwise incomprehensible behaviors and experiences. These stories emerge even when there is little or no logic to them. The left brain's job is to handle storytelling, because it is the home of our language capacities. The left hemisphere carries out abstractions, looking for the commonalities in the objects and scenes it is observing. This story-telling side of the brain relies more on memory and general knowledge than on the precise details of an event for filling in the gaps it encounters. The right brain, by contrast, is more aware of specific details and is much less likely to mistake one event or object for another.[5]

If the left brain constructs stories even in the absence of "facts," we are left to wonder about the validity of any of the stories that we tell ourselves. Some neuroscientists even go so far as to argue that our notions of self-consciousness are constructed realities that give us a false sense of will and choice. They suggest that our experiences of choosing are, in fact, awareness *after* the fact — that we have already decided automatically and unconsciously and only become aware of

5. Daniel L. Schacter, *The Seven Sins of Memory: How the Mind Forgets and Remembers* (Boston: Houghton Mifflin, 2001), 159.

our decisions after they have been made. In his own provocative way, Gazzaniga proclaims, "The left brain weaves its story in order to convince itself and you that it is in full control."[6] He goes even further when he declares, "Biography is fiction. Autobiography is hopelessly inventive."[7]

Whether or not we are willing to go that far, the left hemisphere does provide the words for our stories and has a sense of chronology and time. The right hemisphere in contrast is timeless, living in a kind of constant eternity. But it does accept the job (in most people) of holding together the bigger picture, including the context of what's happening right now. The right hemisphere balances the left hemisphere's nearly unstoppable storytelling by a certain literalness, that is, collecting the details and thereby countering the left hemisphere's propensity to make abstractions and generalize on the basis of categories rather than particular perceptions.[8]

In recent years, the right brain has been romanticized. It has been credited as the source of creativity, and many have prayed for its release from captivity to the overbearing, restrictive left hemisphere. Yet the two hemispheres function as a team, and the right brain has some less noble qualities as well. For instance, while both hemispheres are involved in emotional experience, each "specializes" in particular feelings.[9] The left hemisphere is able to experience joy and happiness, while the right gives us our feelings of anger, fear, and disgust.

Christina Santhouse, the young girl we encountered in the introduction to this volume, now lives with half a brain. The surgery that removed her right hemisphere apparently took place at an early enough age that the left hemisphere was able to learn the tasks that the right brain would normally perform. Such is the wonderful flexibility of the developing brain. Brain cells are "utility players," able to learn different roles in different brain locations, particularly early

6. Gazzaniga, *The Mind's Past*, 25.
7. Ibid., p. 2.
8. Schacter, *The Seven Sins of Memory*, 157–60.
9. Ornstein, *The Right Mind*, 73–75.

in life. The later in life that injury or illness damages a brain, however, the less likely that other neurons can pick up the work of the damaged or missing neurons. So most adults need both hemispheres working and communicating together.

The two hemispheres are partners in our important tasks, jumping into the process at different times and under different circumstances. When we are reading or hearing technical types of work — computer manuals, math books, and, unfortunately, some theology books — the left side of the brain is most active. But when we are reading stories, the right brain joins happily into the task. (The right brain seems to become active in technical reading only if the typeface is artsy!) The left hemisphere is better at processing logical details, interpreting the sequences of time, and providing the words to name things. The right hemisphere, by contrast, grasps the bigger picture, understands the context and can hold several possible meanings "in mind" at the same time. So in a gross oversimplification, we could say that the left hemisphere is creating stories out of the images presented to it by the right hemisphere. But we must have both.

Now That's Funny

Our ability to understand jokes and indirect requests requires the right brain's capacity for understanding multiple meanings. In class one day, a student made this request: "Is it possible to open the door so that we could get some fresh air in here?" Because the colleague with whom I was coteaching this course has the full use of both hemispheres (I presume!), she stood up and opened the door. Now if she had lost the use of certain areas of the cortex in her right hemisphere, she might have responded to that question by simply saying, "Yes. It is possible," and she would have been saying it without a hint of sarcasm. The right hemisphere of her brain would have been unable to hold the multiple meanings of the question together at one time, and she would have likely simply answered the question. Understanding the context and nuances of meanings is critical to interpreting that kind of message, and the right hemisphere shoulders the burden.

Puns and jokes are a good example of this capacity. Puns by definition employ a word with multiple meanings and establish a scenario in which at least two meanings of the word compete.

> Two atoms are walking down the street, when all of a sudden, one atom stops, and says, "Oh no! I think I lost an electron!" So the other one turns to him and asks, "Are you sure?" To which the first one replies, "I'm POSITIVE!"

For this joke to strike us as funny, we must understand some elementary physics, but more important we must grasp two different meanings of the word "positive" at the same time: an expression of certainty and the nature of an electrical charge that results from having more positrons than negatively charged electrons in an atom. The right brain is better at holding onto those multiple meanings of words, while the left brain quickly selects one meaning and rules the others out. As a lover of puns, I am grateful for the present health of my brain's right hemisphere.

It is no wonder that sermons which are explanations of technical theological concepts often don't engage us much. They may only be tapping half the brain, if that. Counseling sessions and classes as well as sermons that deal with images and stories, on the other hand, are more engaging — in part because they are likely to activate more of the brain. When we are truly engaged in hearing — living within the story of another person or within the stories of our faith communities — the experience involves the brain's total participation. Both hemispheres have jumped in and contribute to interpreting the story.

The connection of the right hemisphere to faith may be even more focused than that. Because the right hemisphere (especially the parietal lobe) is responsible for determining our sense of location, our place in the world, Ornstein speculates that the right brain might be the home of our sense of place in the universe — the meaning of life. For all his fear of dichotomania, he is certainly a fan of the right hemisphere![10] We have known for a long time that the right brain is at least a center for images, for play, and for imagining possibility.

We tell stories, and we hear stories. Certainly the way to understand another person, another family, another faith tradition, or another culture is to listen carefully to the stories they tell.

The Brain's Drive to Interpret

The nature of human beings is to explain the way things are. We keep looking for answers to the "why" questions because we cannot make sense of the world and of our place in it without them. Sometimes we figure it out for ourselves, such as when I can't get my car to start on a cold winter morning. I'll make some guess about what's wrong (the engine is too cold, the battery is weak, there is no gas in the tank, or there is ice in the gas line). Then I'll test each possible reason until I discover the one that solves the problem.

Sometimes answers are provided for us, by the stories we tell about our own lives, by the explanations our families give us, or by the answers science or our culture offers us. Sometimes we must find new answers to old or new questions or to situations we've never faced. When all else fails, we construct an explanation or accept one that someone else offers us (particularly some authority like a pastor, therapist, or physician).

This drive to know has been called the "cognitive imperative."[11] This capacity of the brain is very similar to the left hemisphere's interpreter described by Gazzaniga above. We've already noted that when there are gaps in the stories that explain our life experiences, mechanisms or systems in the brain fill in the gaps. But the implication is even larger than simply making stories complete. We cannot tolerate not knowing. Yes, sometimes we crave the experience of mystery — of encountering things we don't understand. That is the other side

---

10. Ibid., 162.
11. Eugene d'Aquili and Andrew B. Newberg, *The Mystical Mind: Probing the Biology of Religious Experience* (Minneapolis: Fortress Press, 1999), 196–97.

of our experience of createdness. But more often, we are unable to live (or at least we experience it that way) without knowing. Our brains are created, or have evolved, to make meaning out of our experiences. This remarkable characteristic of the human brain is likely a key capacity that sets humans apart from all other species. Large gaps in what we know about ourselves, about the world, about God, demand that we look for explanations. In the face of some experiences, we even create memories to satisfy our need to know. We hold on to stories that have explanatory power.

Parenthetically, this dimension of the human brain has given rise to both religion and science. While a broad discussion of the relationship between these two broad human endeavors is well beyond the scope of this volume, let me at least suggest that, while theology and science have distinct differences in both method and content, they are ultimately both driven by the human need to know — to comprehend the world in which we live and the nature of our own existence.

A further extension of the construction of a personal sense of self involves feelings of uniqueness. Some experiences that initially produce feelings of shame or helplessness, of victimhood, can result in a feeling of set-apartness, of having aspects of oneself that few others in the world share — in short, the experience of being different. Recovering alcoholics, for instance, frequently construct their personal identities around their addictions to alcohol. Likewise, some former victims of sexual or physical abuse describe themselves as "survivors," knowing that only other survivors can really appreciate what that means.

Such self-identification serves powerful healing purposes. Acknowledging the painful stories that have been part of one's personal history and naming the wounds inflicted on oneself when particularly vulnerable is a critical part of the healing process for most kinds of trauma. Patient companionship with persons, particularly during times of discovery, is a mark of faithfulness. At the same time there are at least two risks that accompany this identification. First, victims may begin to experience themselves primarily, or nearly entirely, on the basis of their victimization. While that self-identification often understandably becomes a focus of one's attention during and immediately after discovery of the memory, it can also blind persons to other vital and positive dimensions of who they are. In the very act of joining a survivor in the process of liberation from the sense of defectiveness, helplessness, or woundedness he or she may have been experiencing for years, an obsessive focus on that dimension of personal history can reenslave the victim. Identification of self as a survivor is an important transitional step, and any caregiver or friend must respect the timing that is unique to each survivor. Ultimately, however, true healing results when former victims are able to regain a sense of their own fullness and competence.

This notion of survivor identification as a transitional identity points us to the second risk. Even for persons who embrace the breadth of experiences they have had in life, continued identification as a survivor or as an alcoholic may serve to undermine a sense of growth and transformation. True alcoholics may in fact never be able to drink alcohol without risk of relapse; knowing the power of one's own addictions and vulnerabilities is central to appropriate care for oneself and to making healthier choices. Sexual abuse survivors may always struggle with interpersonal, particularly intimate, relationships. Healing calls for a balance between confronting the reality of limitations with hope for change, so that one's addictions or history of abuse do not become the center of one's identity.

Story and Self

Recognizing that we write our own life stories might at first reading seem a rather arrogant proposition. We more often think about telling a story that is already there, encoded in our brains. We're just reporting what has already taken place, except of course when we are telling a story in fun, or repeating a folktale we have heard. But just like we do with memories, we select the stories that we remember and include in the narrative of our lives. We select, too, which details we encode and which we retrieve. There are too many events and too many memories to include them all in the story of our lives. We must choose selectively.

Telling a story is always a process of interpretation and selection. We are always bringing our own experience, our own history, and our own spin on things when we tell our stories. This is distinctly different from reading a written biography. It's much more like picking out the events in our lives that best represent what most of the other events in life have been like. Our brains automatically select and remember stories that represent the themes of life, almost like some cosmic editor dropping out the material in a story that is redundant, boring, or trivial. Psychologist McAdams says it this way:

> Fashioning a personal myth is not an exercise in narcissistic delusion, or a paranoid attempt to establish oneself as God. Instead, defining the self through myth may be seen as an ongoing act of psychological and social *responsibility*. Because our world can no longer tell us who we are and how we should live, we must figure it out on our own.[12]

Perhaps it is clearer to describe our role in self-authoring as creativity or imagination. This process is quite familiar to us in our biblical tradition. We need only read and compare the four Gospels to notice that some stories appear in one or two of the Gospels and not in others. Even when a story appears in more than one, it may be in different places in different Gospels. The ones that are there are there for a reason — they give us a particular angle on the story, a particular dimension of Jesus' life, death, and resurrection. So in Matthew we have a picture of Jesus as the fulfillment of the Hebrew Scriptures. In Luke we have a picture of Jesus the healer. In John, we see Christ as eternal Logos present in the world. And the stories in the Gospels give evidence of their overarching truths. A New Testament colleague tells me that the only story that appears similarly in all four Gospels

---

12. McAdams, *Stories We Live By,* 35.

is the story of the feeding of the five thousand. Surely this beloved story speaks to our own spiritual hunger and God's extravagant grace in nourishing our souls as well as our bodies.

In a similar manner, the events that we remember from our own narratives and that we tell are there for a reason. We need to make sense of life, to have some sense of its meaning and coherence. The story needs to hang together. We select, more or less automatically, the stories that represent significant unfolding themes in our lives. Often one remembered story stands in for many other similar stories that we do not recall so explicitly. Stories that connect with other experiences in our lives are more likely to be remembered — and more likely to be included in the stories we tell of our own lives.

Narrative Voices

Early in the twentieth century Worcester State Hospital chaplain Anton Boisen, the grandparent of the modern pastoral care movement and clinical pastoral education, brought theology students into mental hospitals to learn about mental illness firsthand, not from psychiatry books or systematic theologies, but from persons actually suffering with emotional disorders. From this work, and from his own personal experiences of profound mental illness, Boisen first referred to the sufferer as "the living human document."[13] Early twentieth-century seminarians attended to hospital patients and learned from them. Listening to those who were distressed, pastors-to-be learned about the meaning of chaos, disordered minds, suffering, healing, and wholeness. Pastors began studying persons instead of merely reading books about persons. It's a bit like getting to know God firsthand rather than relying on books about God.

In 1984, pastoral theologian Charles Gerkin developed Boisen's central notion in a pivotal book titled appropriately *The Living*

---

13. E. B. Holifield, "Anton Boisen," in Rodney J. Hunter, ed., *Dictionary of Pastoral Care and Counseling* (Nashville: Abingdon Press, 1990), 104–5.

Human Document.[14] Gerkin attempted to relate theology and psychology more deeply by arguing that practitioners of pastoral care and counseling could use methods of interpretation like those of biblical scholars as they struggled to understand the stories of suffering persons. He contended that we could learn about persons most deeply and effectively by listening to their stories — not just the words that were spoken, but the themes and nuances behind the stories. In fact, Gerkin claimed that we could approach the stories of people who came to us with tools that paralleled the tools of biblical and literary studies. In Gerkin's work, pastoral care and counseling found a voice anchoring those functions within the field of narrative psychotherapy. The methods of pastoral care and counseling moved closer to the methods in which clergy have been trained for decades — the methodologies of hermeneutics. We could study people in some of the same ways we study the Bible.

Narrative methods have emerged not only in pastoral care but in other disciplines as well, particularly in psychology. At the beginning of this chapter, McAdams reminded us of the central place personal storytelling has in the ways we form our individual identities. Of course we become a self before we have words to tell stories — or at least we begin to become a self. But constructing a life story is an inevitable, critical, and lifelong task that brings each of us into being as a unique self. We are the stories we tell.

Narrative approaches to pastoral care and counseling have found fertile soil among groups that were marginalized by earlier approaches to care, mental health, and theology itself. Pastoral theologian and pastoral counselor Ed Wimberly has argued in *African American Pastoral Care* that narrative theology and narrative approaches to pastoral care are the most culturally common dimensions in work with African American persons and families.[15] African

---

14. Charles Gerkin, *The Living Human Document: Re-Visioning Pastoral Counseling in a Hermeneutical Mode* (Nashville: Abingdon Press, 1984).

15. Edward P. Wimberly, *African American Pastoral Care* (Nashville: Abingdon Press, 1991), 9.

American experiences are best understood in the telling of personal and communal stories and in the relating of stories to the biblical narratives. Pastoral theologian Christie Neuger has persuasively argued for the centrality of narrative pastoral care approaches in work with women, particularly victims of domestic violence and sexual abuse.[16]

And stories are not merely about the past. We tell stories about the future as well — those anticipated scenarios that are a by-product of our symbolizing brains. Pastoral theologian Andrew Lester has expanded our understanding of narrative in pastoral counseling by arguing persuasively for the power of "future stories" in providing care.[17] He urges us to listen to the imagined stories of the future that members of our congregations or our clients bring with them. How we imagine the future is at least as important as what we remember from the past. We already know that memory and imagination overlap, but here we extend that notion a step further. Memory is our primary means of recording what has already happened. But we also are constantly writing stories about what lies ahead of us. We all live with story plots that extend for months and years beyond today. And just like many of our stories of the past, our stories of the future are not often spoken out loud.

Lester observes that many of our counseling theories, particularly those grounded in psychoanalysis, have emphasized the power of past stories — the ways the wounds and neglects of childhood continue to influence the ways we think, feel, and behave today. Other counseling theories, such as cognitive or family systems approaches, have emphasized the significance of current stories. We attend to the thoughts persons are having at this point in time and to the other people in their lives to understand how they contribute to the suffering now. We also anticipate the ways those thoughts and relationships might be reconfigured to help in healing. Lester makes an effective case for

---

16. Christie Neuger, *Counseling Women: A Narrative, Pastoral Approach* (Minneapolis: Fortress Press, 2001).

17. Andrew Lester, *Hope in Pastoral Care and Counseling* (Louisville: Westminster John Knox Press, 1995).

the counselor's attention to imagined future stories, our anticipations and images of the open-ended future to which God calls us. It is often our future stories that bring us suffering, yet our future stories can also bring us hope. We return to this understanding later in this chapter and again in chapter 5.

Contributions of Narrative Methods

A narrative approach to pastoral care and counseling (and to other practices such as spiritual direction) provides significant implications for structuring the care we offer.

1. One of the consequences of the shift in pastoral care and counseling's focus to story is the move away from a static (or medical) model of diagnosis, of pigeonholing, to a more dynamic attention to the unique stories of individuals and of families. When we can avoid — or at least delay — categorizing persons according to some set of preestablished categories — either psychological or theological — we are operating in a more genuinely pastoral modality. When we can step aside from what we *expect* to hear from "someone like this," we are able to listen to the particularity of the person who actually does sit across the room from us. When we can allow ourselves to be surprised, then the stories we hear from people can be truly new and truly revealing. *We listen to stories because people are unique and because people grow and change.*

2. Listening to stories can give us a deep sense of the meaning that people have made of their lives. The events they include, the ones they omit, and the inevitable embellishments and discounts they make can help us appreciate how the world is constructed for persons who seek our care. Harvard psychiatrist John Ratey recommends that psychotherapists abandon the familiar inquiry, "How do you feel?" and ask instead the question, "How do you know the world?"[18]

---

18. John J. Ratey, *A User's Guide to the Brain: Perception, Attention, and the Four Theaters of the Brain* (New York: First Vintage Books, 2002), 7, 8.

We human beings are built to organize and structure our worlds in ways that make sense, that hold together internally, and that give us bearings in an otherwise incomprehensible world. As we noted above, thanks to the cognitive imperative and the left hemisphere's interpreter, we cannot not make sense of the world around us. We have already observed that this same impulse may lead some people to fill in the blanks with stories that do not fit the facts — sometimes even stories that are destructive. Here we look at the ways our need to know gives us life and health. Our very emotional, spiritual, and even physical survival depends on it. While some aspects of our meaning-worlds might puzzle us or disconcert us, the whole must make sense if we are to survive. *We tell stories to discover and define who we are.*

3. A third value of storytelling as a central act of pastoral care is that it offers us opportunities to transcend cultural differences in ways that our culturally biased theories cannot. So many of the cultural theories that continue to inform pastoral care are culturally limited, that is, they reflect the cultural values of nineteenth-century Vienna or of North American, English-speaking Caucasian peoples, and don't translate well to persons of other traditions.[19] Most of us have encountered a small culture shock when talking with a person of a culture different from our own. The values are different, the rules are different, and, at the heart of the matter, the social worlds in which we live are different. That is, the "way the world just is" to a person of another culture may be shockingly strange to us. When our central purpose in listening to another is to tell and hear stories, we open up ways of understanding that contribute to deepened awareness and may help us avoid the ethnocentrism that characterizes so much of our experience. Because stories carry the meaning of cultural value systems, this approach is more promising for cross-cultural pastoral counseling than many other approaches. *We tell stories to let another know who we are.*

---

19. Emanuel Lartey, *In Living Colour: An Intercultural Approach to Pastoral Care and Counselling* (London: Cassell, 1997), viii.

4. Attending to story offers us a way to listen that applies equally well at many levels of relationship, offering access not only to people's personal stories but stories of their faith traditions and of their cultures. These higher-order stories serve at least two functions for us. First, cultural and faith stories provide the raw material for our personal stories, the heroes and villains, the miniplots and literary forms that we make use of to build our own stories. The sports heroes, the politicians, the actors who populate our cultural worlds provide multiple images and roles that find their way into the personal stories that each of us composes. The mothers, fathers, grandparents, aunts, uncles, brothers, and sisters who share our family stories are also characters in the plots of our own lives that give us models and help shape who we are.

Second, because stories are critical to our identity, the stories we share with others create and strengthen our shared identity with others. We are united with others who tell the same stories of faith or who recite the same history of a particular people. We name and deepen our shared identity with others as we remember the critical steps on the journey to this time and place. These stories help us understand where we fit in our communities and where we fit in the world. *We tell stories in order to belong.*

Families

Our families are vital places of belonging — and therefore of stories. For most of us, our families are not only the settings of our birth and our genesis. They represent the network of caring relationships within which we first became who we are. Much has been said and written about the critical role the family plays in the first years of life. But for a moment, consider the role the family plays in the *stories* of our lives. We don't develop the capacity for words until a year-and-a-half into life, so our first experiences of ourselves are wordless.[20] We experience

---

20. Daniel N. Stern, *The Interpersonal World of the Infant: A View from Psychoanalysis and Developmental Psychology* (New York: Basic Books, 1985), 6; McAdams, *Stories We Live By,* 35.

the bodily sensations of emotion, pleasure, and discomfort. We learn to recognize the people in our lives, and we begin to learn the basic skills of life. But because we have no words, we have as yet no story of our own. Even memory at the start of life is something of a mystery. As adults we have no narrative memories of those first years of life.

So our families are the tellers and holders of our stories from our earliest days. We learn later in life from others what life was like for us during infancy. The stories of our birth are particularly poignant. Our birth stories help us understand who we were to become and what roles we were to play. We begin to suspect whose place in the family we were to take, perhaps because we were given their name or frequently told how much we are like them. There is a deep hunger for those stories. My own children would have listened to stories of their births and early years for hours on end if we had had the stamina to keep telling them. We would tell one or two stories, and they would beg for another. We long to hear the stories of our entry into the world first because they tell us often more than any other stories about who we are. We also yearn to hear them because we have no immediate memory of them ourselves.

In chapter 2 we spoke of the brain's capacity to treat imagined stories as real — to absorb them, particularly with frequent rehearsal — so they are vivid and clear. It is difficult to comprehend that we may have been in no real position to form those memories for ourselves. They are so vivid and so persistent that we are certain of their truth.

Stories and Communities

We tell stories of God and God's people most often within our communities of faith. When we gather for worship, we come for the purpose of storytelling and story listening at least as much as for any other reason. We come to listen and we come to tell. "Tell me the stories of Jesus," we sing. But we also sing "I Love to Tell the

Story." Hearing and telling the stories of faith reinforce our memories of those stories. Those stories draw us in again as we experience them in the presence of others. Once more, memory and imagination work hand in hand in this partnership of storytelling. We remember and we relive the stories of our faith.

Imaginatively participating in a story we are hearing is a consequence of our capacity for empathy. The ability to walk in another's shoes or see the world through another's eyes is central to being human. Listening to a story in worship (or watching a play or reading a novel) calls on the same capacities we employ in listening to others in other settings. Only now the arousal systems in our brains are activated, our expectancy is heightened, and the brain's prefrontal cortex focuses our attention. Once again we are the beneficiaries of brains that make empathic participation possible. As we described in chapter 1, our brains first imagine ourselves performing the acts or behaviors we are observing. That is, we are mentally rehearsing the same performance the characters in the story are enacting. We identify ourselves with them. For a time at least, we have entered another world. We are participating imaginatively in another's story. At the same time, these acts or behaviors also activate portions of the brain that are responsible for providing us with a sense of boundaries — of being a self separate from other selves.

Psychologists have long observed the rapid communication of strong feelings within groups of people (and many other species, for that matter). In its most primitive form they refer to this automatic communication as "emotional contagion."[21] Strong feelings are catching. Unless we are inhibited by brain injury or by earlier emotional experiences, we cannot avoid feeling the pain or joy of another. While we are particularly susceptible to emotional contagion in infancy, the brain never outgrows its ability to mirror the feelings of another. As the brain matures, the prefrontal lobes develop and

---

21. Stephanie D. Preston and Frans B. M. de Waal, "Empathy: Its Ultimate and Proximate Bases," *Behavioral and Brain Sciences* 25 (February 2002).

enable us to exercise some control over those reactive emotional processes and refine our responses. As the brain develops its capacities for emotional self-regulation and for language, the power of stories to engage our feeling selves emerges. We no longer have to hear or see someone crying to trigger similar feelings in ourselves. Hearing or reading about someone else's suffering can stimulate those feelings. Stories become a critical tool in organizing our experiences of the world. And these empathic abilities of the brain create and deepen our sense of belonging.

In chapter 4 we look more closely at the ways the brain participates in ritual experiences. Suffice it to say at this point that stories that are read and enacted within a worship setting create a common narrative experience that deepens a sense of connection with others in the group. As our brains imaginatively reconstruct the stories of our faith, they engage us in a world shared by others around us. The association areas of the cortex responsible for the boundaries around self loosen their hold on us ever so slightly, enabling us to feel a sense of unity not possible in the day-to-day rush of life's activities.[22]

It is sad but true that, as a people, we no longer share the stories of faith as widely and as deeply as we once did. Fewer people sitting in our pews on a Sunday morning know the stories of Jesus, let alone the stories of David, Ruth, Naomi, and Abraham. These stories compete for our attention with (and too often are much less familiar than) stories of Harry Potter and Luke Skywalker. Biblical literacy is on the decline, even among students enrolling in seminary. Adults and children are coming to our churches with only a rudimentary knowledge of a few biblical stories, if any knowledge at all. So one of the central roles of the church today is to tell those stories over and over again, in ways that capture the attention of those who have not heard them. Our worship and our pastoral care all eventually depend on our religious education and our evangelism.

---

22. d'Aquili and Newberg, *The Mystical Mind*, 112.

This practice of storytelling in the church points us to one last implication of storytelling.

5. Finally, this multiple-level approach to stories leads to an important relationship for pastoral care and counseling — the possibility for the *intersection of stories* — or what pastoral theologian Herbert Anderson and liturgical theologian Ed Foley refer to as "weaving together the human and the divine stories."[23] Some of us may understand the biblical tradition as human beings telling stories to make sense of their encounters with God. Others of us may see God's storytelling as a divine self-revelation. Either way, human beings have connected with those texts for centuries because they have sensed in them profound truths about the deepest structures of life; about its source and its destiny; about its questions, its meanings, and its purpose. We have found our own experiences mirrored and reinterpreted in the light of those stories and have found ourselves drawn into communities of faith with others who find themselves reflected in those same stories.

We tell our own stories. Our communities tell and retell their stories. God's story is told and retold. And because God loves a good story, we find our own stories deepened and reinterpreted in the context of those larger stories. This notion of intersecting stories, or weaving together the personal and the divine stories, is a profoundly significant and complex notion. There is a way in which it is a mystery. At the same time it is a central purpose for our worship and for our pastoral care and counseling.

Crossing the Intersection

How does this intersection take place? What must happen for personal and larger narratives to interact with and change each other?

We find our own stories within the biblical narrative. We are mirrored there, because the stories of God's people are our own stories

---

23. Herbert Anderson and Edward Foley, *Mighty Stories, Dangerous Rituals: Weaving Together the Human and the Divine* (Los Angeles: Jossey-Bass, 1998), 36–54.

written in all capital letters. We have experienced the impulsiveness of Peter and can even admit to times we have denied who we truly are. We see ourselves in Moses' fear of leadership, in David's lust, and in Mary's deep grief for a dying son. We see glimpses of our best selves and our worst selves in Paul and in Sarah. We see our own struggles to relate to God played out in the stories of Martin Luther and Teresa of Avila. When we sit down in the theater of our historic faith, we find our own lives being played out on the stage.

Our contemporary North American society suffers from both too many guides to living and too few. McAdams says it this way: "Because our world can no longer tell us who we are and how we should live, we must figure it out on our own."[24] It is perhaps a mixed blessing that we have so many options about how to live our lives. We are no longer locked into particular roles as men and women, as persons of faith. By the same token, no longer is it an easy matter to determine how we are to behave. Freedom always brings with it responsibility. We no longer all share the same story in the ways our grandparents and our parents did. In Chicago, it is nearly as likely that we will live next door to a Muslim as it is that we will live next door to a Christian or a Jew. And even among Christians, there is generally a much wider range of lifestyle choices and beliefs available to us than to our parents and grandparents. Nonetheless, with apologies to Dr. McAdams, stories of the Christian faith can in fact help us figure out who we are.

Our personal stories and the divine story intersect in a second way. Larger stories of faith provide the overarching themes we use to interpret our own lives. The New Testament, for instance, teaches us about the paradoxical nature of life and shows us that, in order to live, we must first die. To be first we must be last; to show love to God we must show love to the "least of these"; to be truly wealthy we must give away all that we have. The Hebrew Scriptures offer us stories of a God who liberates us from slavery, who goes before us as

---

24. McAdams, *Stories We Live By,* 35.

smoke in the daylight and fire at night. The ways we understand our own lives are the products of the overarching stories that we use to frame them.

This renewed emphasis on storytelling has at least one central implication. We pastors and chaplains, pastoral counselors and spiritual directors, we seminary students and theological educators must consistently be immersed in the stories that shape our communities of faith — those stories most notably present to us in the biblical record, but also those unfolding stories of the church and of persons of faith who write for us or speak to us. If we *are* the stories we tell, and if we belong to each other and to God through the stories we share, then retelling those stories for ourselves as well as for others is key to the pastoral task. And even beyond that, our immersion in those stories should be multidimensional. That is, we should honor and exercise our biblical scholarship, but we should also be immersed in our faith in worship, in prayer, in devotional exercise in ways that allow our own deeper experiences to be caught up and reinterpreted in the light of the biblical text.

Such formation must include critical appraisal of the stories we are telling and hearing, for many stories are destructive and disempowering, as we shall see below. Finding a Bible verse or injunction that gives us direction for each pain or dilemma that we experience or that a hurting parishioner or client brings to us is also not the answer. Nevertheless, we need to hear and tell the stories of faith in the physical presence of those with whom we share that faith.

Theory of Change

One of the key questions that must be asked of any approach to understanding human development focuses on the approach's *theory of change*. That is, how does this approach suggest human beings can become different from who they are or how they are living? What qualities or conditions are necessary for persons to be healed or transformed?

1. Narrative theory and theology suggest at least three conditions for change:

In the first place, the very *telling of our stories may be healing.*[25] Since storytelling is the way we make meaning of our lives, then telling our story to another human being brings that story to life once again. When we tell our story to someone who has never heard it, in a sense we are telling that story for the first time. It is reassuring: our own lives make sense all over again. In chapter 2 we observed that our memories may not last forever in our brains. Memories may fade over time or disappear altogether. When we tell our stories again, we are re-membering them ourselves and keeping them alive, maintaining their power. We are reminding ourselves about who we are.

Sometimes just the opposite is true. Some stories are painful and intrusive. Their persistence and unwelcome presence do not bring healing or wholeness. Instead, they continuously re-wound us. Victims of sexual abuse, combat veterans, and victims of domestic violence often find memories painful and troubling. By telling those stories, victims can weaken the stories' power over them. Untold stories and secrets can harm and destroy more quickly than stories that have been shared. For some persons, this may mean bringing to light stories that have been too painful to tell, plots that reveal aspects of themselves that they have not yet been able to tolerate, or stories that do not fit with the life stories they thought they were writing. Telling the story may provide healing by granting access to their own life narratives — those aspects of the story that have been cut off, that have not been available to complete the story. We have this need to know, as you remember, and stories that are kept at arm's length invite even more destructive stories to take their place.

2. A second way storytelling makes human change possible involves *rewriting the story.* At first glance, that possibility sounds like inviting delusion or denial — almost as though we could customize or edit our life stories. But any time we tell a story, we are interpreting

25. Schacter, *The Seven Sins of Memory,* 171; Neuger, *Counseling Women,* 65–92; McAdams, *Stories We Live By,* 31–33.

the events that we are reporting. Even when we select which events to include in a story, and which to exclude, we have already begun to determine the meaning of the story. Pastoral care and counseling as well as spiritual direction, therefore, often involve helping persons put life events into new perspectives, including different parts of the story, making different sense of it all. Sensitive listening to stories along with careful questions about puzzles or missing pieces can open the possibility of hidden dimensions of the story that may radically change a story's meaning.

Counseling couples in conflict is one of the best examples of this process. Partners bring their own life stories to the wedding altar as they begin a new story together. For most of us, those anticipated stories are full of hope and promise. But inevitably a chapter appears in the couple's story that doesn't live up to the original script. A miscarriage or serious illness, an affair, long periods of neglect, a business failure — these are just a few examples of events that may become unwanted episodes in the story of life together. When partners withdraw physically or emotionally from each other, they may be writing stories of their own — without consulting the coauthor.

Part of the process of healing for such a couple is a rewriting of the story — past, present, or future. Elsewhere we have referred to this process as "promising again."[26] Sometimes the story of the present must be revised. "What I understood as his neglect of me turns out to be his fear of failing to provide for me. We must talk openly about money so that we can share a realistic picture of our financial circumstances." Or, "What I thought was her angry withholding of affection turned out to be her fear about her health. I will be open to hearing her anxiety rather than judging her behavior."

At other times past stories are rewritten. "I was afraid he must be having an affair, but it turned out he really did have too much work to do." "Though I thought she was turning out to be just as neglectful as her mother, I learned instead that she was distracted

---

26. Herbert Anderson, David Hogue, and Marie McCarthy, *Promising Again* (Louisville: Westminster John Knox Press, 1995).

by worries about her work." Even tragic new twists in the plot of stories require that we grieve the loss of earlier plans and move toward acceptance of new directions in life. Sometimes future stories must be rewritten. The infertile couple who had dreamed of biological family. The just-retired couple with plans to see the world must now confront a husband's debilitating stroke. Sometimes future stories become more hopeful. The AIDS husband whose remission requires a couple to rewrite a longer story together. The infertile couple who adopt a child and then find themselves pregnant. When we rewrite our stories, we change who we know ourselves to be.

We must also acknowledge that cultural stories are frequently destructive narratives for persons who are marginalized by the tone and outcome of those stories. Rewriting cultural stories is a daunting task. Neuger has described the process of "deconstructive listening" as a response to persons who suffer under such stories. Deconstructive listening involves three steps: externalizing the problem ("The problem is not me"), naming the problem, and seeking the "unique outcomes."[27] Key to the third step is a careful attending to exceptions to the dominant story, noting the ways a counselee has functioned that undermine the dominant narrative which he or she has constructed about him or herself. Deconstructive listening involves carefully subverting stories which dictate or limit roles and opportunities for certain groups of people. The counselor looks for small examples of resistance to images of passivity or helplessness, or evidence of care of self or resourcefulness. By pointing them out, the counselor can begin to call into question the validity of some cultural stories and help loosen the hold they have over persons on the margins. Such freedom can then invite the rewriting of empowering stories.

3. When rewriting our stories takes a radical turn, we sometimes *discover a new story* that redefines life. Of course, we don't randomly pick a new story from some cosmic bookshelf and recast life within

---

27. Neuger, *Counseling Women*, 90–92.

the pages of that new book. However, sometimes in the retelling of a story, over time, that story may become so radically different from the life story that we previously understood, the new story is experienced as restructuring life. It is something like putting new wine in old wineskins. As the wine ferments, the old containers are not strong enough to hold the new wine and they burst. It is an experience of transformation of life's deepest structures. This is one way for us to understand the experience of conversion. As the themes of life are transformed, its meaning and purpose are altered or discovered, and persons genuinely find themselves to be "new creations." Whether such an occurrence takes place suddenly or over time, we may well understand the experience as discovering a new story for one's life.

Paul talks of his experience of the "old humanity" and the "new humanity" following his dramatic conversion on the road to Damascus. Within the Christian tradition, the adult rite of baptism underscores this dramatic, discontinuous break with the old life as old garments are exchanged for new white ones. For most of us, though, spiritual growth involves putting together the old familiar stories in ways that make them truly new. We look back over the stories of our lives and discover the ways in which God was present — caring, seeking us out, and even guiding our way.

Tall Tales and Fractured Fables

There are many ways stories can go astray as well as ways stories can hold us and heal us. We'll call two of those ways "tall tales and fractured fables." Their meaning is self-evident at one level. Tall tales suggest those more elaborate exaggerations of life stories, or very careful, selective editing of stories that place the hero or heroine in a unique or special position. They are the stuff of which legends are made. They include those birth stories that suggest a child's special gifts or unique connection with another member of the family. They include stories of unusual exploits in childhood, either good or destructive, that signal the expectations families have of their children.

They often omit events that don't quite fit the image the family has of the person in question or that the person has of himself or herself.

Because stories often invite their own embellishment over time, tall tales characterize most of our life stories to a certain extent. At their best, they signal the realistic and valued qualities that a person brings to life. They may even contribute to a sense of optimism about the future and generally enhance mental health.[28] At their worst, however, they cover uncertainty about personal worth or produce drivenness in the person who fears loss of life itself if the image is not maintained. While both men and women are vulnerable to tall tales, they are more typically the domain of men. Tall tales may be inevitable, but in time, they also call for review and evaluation.

Fractured fables, on the other hand, suggest stories of brokenness or wounding. "Fractured" describes the story itself. It fails to provide the coherent meaning structure the left brain requires to comprehend its place in the world. This story may be radically disconnected from the predominant stories that shape self-understanding, so at odds with the ideal self a person imagines that it must be denied or forgotten. At other times the brain has failed to hold on to memories, and gaps appear in stories so individuals wander through life without a sense of identity and without the capacity to connect to life's other stories. The story doesn't work. It doesn't do what the brain needs it to do.

"Fractured" can also refer to the storyteller. Life stories that include emotional, physical, or sexual abuse; children who seem to have been born to fulfill someone else's life story; or children who have faced unexpected loss may well come to us with fractured fables. Where fractured fables reveal the tragic realities of a person's life, where they offer explanation for suffering, where they point to the cause of pain or dysfunction in life, fractured fables can become avenues to healing. Where they dominate the tone and form of life's

---

28. Schacter, *The Seven Sins of Memory*, 194.

story itself, they can hold persons prisoner to the suffering which they originally engendered.

The notion of fractured fables also acknowledges that cultural stories are often disempowering, particularly for women and persons of color. All too frequently the larger cultural stories (including biblical stories) serve the ends of sexism, racism, and heterosexism, deepening the marginalization of those excluded from privilege. Historical criticism has made explicit the ways persons of privilege have in fact served as the keepers and tellers of cultural stories and so ensured their status is maintained. The effectiveness of stories in shaping identity is indeed so strong that storytellers are in positions of great power.

While these two types of story may look quite different, both call for pastoral responses that invite reauthoring, or at least a more complete discovery of life's stories. More important, they call for weaving together the human and divine stories. Our biblical tradition speaks profoundly to the experiences both of specialness and of suffering that these story types suggest. What follows is an example of the possible intersection of biblical and personal stories in ways that could promote self-reflective reappraisal.

The tall-tale paradigm suggests an experience of specialness, of uniqueness, of chosenness that becomes either self-buttressing or that leads to superiority and domination of others. This may be true whether the tall tale supports a giftedness or an experience of exquisite suffering. What results is a deep sense of privilege or entitlement, or worship of self and position. Others are now in this world to serve *my* needs, whether that is because of my strengths, abilities, or position, or because of my pain. The stories of ancient Israel and its leaders, as well as stories of the early Christian church as chosen people, demonstrate to us in paradigmatic ways the potential consequences of such stories. One interpretation of that history demonstrates this very dangerous consequence of tall tales — *we can forget what we are chosen for.* Rather than a place of unbridled privilege, what Israel and the later church were offered was a place of witness and service. If we discover that God's covenants are designed to witness to God's intent for the *whole* world, and to serve God in the world, then the stories of our occasional self-aggrandizement, our expectations that we can be exempt from consequences, demonstrate the dangers of separating uniqueness from the rightful purpose of that chosenness. Such a story might well serve as a broader frame of reference for pastor and person, honoring the giftedness of persons while looking consistently for how gifts can be understood within the broader context of God's story.

Fractured fables also have their counterparts in the biblical text. For Christians, the central paradigm of Christ's death and resurrection serves as a reminder of a truth to which Jesus was witness — that is, that suffering and death are not the final word. That out of our suffering can issue new life. That even in God's apparent abandonment of us, God holds an open-ended future for us. Rather than offering an easy lesson or a trite response to a suffering person, such stories can sustain both pastor and person while together they await the hope that can come only in the midst of suffering.

Being and Doing

In the midst of our appreciation of the central place of storytelling we must note at least one limitation of a purely narrative approach to pastoral counseling. My comments are intended to put storytelling into some perspective and to set the stage for the chapter that follows.

As powerful as words are, they are also limited. Storytelling, to the extent that it is limited to words, may not go far enough. Stories are not only to be told and retold, they are also to be lived. In that sense, stories are more like scripts than like novels. Any encounter that engages only our brains (or more specifically the interpreter in the left hemisphere of the neocortex of the brain) is incomplete. If we limit our spiritual practices to thoughts and feelings and ignore behaviors, then we are falling prey to suspicion of any experiences that cannot be put into words — and we are expecting words to do work of which they are not fully capable. To the degree that we demand to understand before we act, we are overlooking the ineffable, and we may be refusing to appreciate the activity of the Holy Spirit. To the extent that we separate inward conviction from external action, we are engaging in a dualism that does not do justice to the broader scope of the biblical tradition or to our experience as persons of faith. What is called for is a theory of change that includes *enactment* or *embodiment,* for a faith that participates in the Word becoming flesh. We are called to *do* as well as to *be.*

A paradox in this argument will sound familiar to many. Echoes from the early church appear in the counterpoints of Paul's letter to the Romans and James's letter. Paul's clear declaration of justification by faith alone (Rom. 3:28) bumps up against its counterpoint — faith without works is dead (James 2:20). For the writer of that work, in fact, faith is completed, or made perfect, in action. Some dilemmas never go away! It was, of course, this dilemma that helped to launch the Reformation. "Faith alone" served as a motto that stood firmly over against the church's abuses of penitential acts. Our Protestant forebears were not kindly disposed toward the embodied rituals of the church. We revisit that discussion in the next chapter.

Authors and Actors

The second dilemma is of even more interest to our current discussion. None of us is merely an author of our personal stories. We are all actors, even stars in our own productions. We not only cowrite the life stories that we tell; we produce, direct, and star in those stories. Such awareness radically shifts the meaning of storytelling, because the author writes not for another, but for herself or himself.

Among the many implications of this identification of the author with the actor is the necessity of performing. We cannot stop at writing the story. We are called to act as well as to author. Historically, some approaches to pastoral counseling have seemed deliberately to avoid interest in what people do, and there has been reason for that.

The history of "pastoral conversations" from the church's history before the twentieth century was more often a form of moral discourse, persuading and directing care receivers in their rightful duties.[29] Since Sigmund Freud broadened our understanding of the unconscious and awakened our awareness of people's hidden motives (not unknown, by the way, to many biblical authors), most of the helping professions turned to a more *eductive* form of care. Rather than telling people who seek our care what to do, pastors and other helpers began exploring people's experiences and feelings, drawing out the answers to questions rather than providing answers. Pastors began encouraging self-exploration and self-awareness as primary goals of the pastoral counseling process. So the focus of pastoral care in the twentieth century shifted from doing to feeling, from behavior to attitude.

The pastoral counseling movement struggles again with the problematic relationship between being and doing. At times it sounds like a chicken-and-egg argument, going something like, "Which comes first — the change in attitude or the change in behavior?" The biblical writers seem at times to suggest that attitudes precede and are more important than behaviors, so that Jesus says, "It is not what goes into the mouth that defiles a person [it is not the failure to perform the ritual action that condemns], but it is what comes out of the mouth that defiles [his or her speech and attitudes]" (Matt. 15:11, comments added). Or we could refer to qualities that are considered consequences of attitude change, the fruits of the Spirit (Gal. 5:22, 23) and Jesus' assurance that his disciples would be able to tell who his other disciples were "by their fruits" (Matt. 7:16, 20). Clearly Jesus (and the prophets of the Hebrew Scriptures) valued inner attitude over behaviors or rituals that were disconnected from inner experience.

Regardless of which comes first, the attitude or the behavior, what the biblical record does seem to proclaim is the deep relationship

---

29. William A. Clebsch and Charles R. Jaekle, *Pastoral Care in Historical Perspective* (New York: Harper Torchbooks, 1964), 49–51.

between inner conviction and outer behavior. There may well be a discrepancy between how we judge those acts — "for the Lord does not see as mortals see; they look on the outward appearance, but the Lord looks on the heart" (1 Sam. 16:7). But a common understanding is that new life and changed behaviors go together. What this suggests is that pastoral counseling that fails to attend to the "fruits of the Spirit" misses the integrity of human experience.

We observed in chapters 1 and 2 that our brains are constantly attending to the position and state of our bodies as well as to the world around us. We also learned that mirror and motor neurons in the brain rehearse the movements that we are observing even when we are not performing those actions, thoughts, or feelings ourselves. Our brains evolved to know most importantly where things are and what they are,[30] including the position and movement our own bodies made in order to observe them.[31] So our brains are modeled on action and movement, on location and space. Thinking and feeling themselves emerge from the body's experience of itself acting.

Our discussion of memory in chapter 2 reminded us that the brain is a vast network of constantly changing networks of neurons. Experience transforms the complex synaptic connections that are the foundation of memory itself. So the brain is constantly rewiring itself to adapt to new information. Practice may not always make perfect, but it does change things. Both our stories and our actions are central players in this drama of brain reconstruction.

Storytelling is not new. It is as old as language itself and may even precede it in human evolution. Stories both reclaim and deepen our memories, and storytelling is certainly not new to the church. The "discovery" that telling stories is often a healing experience is old news. Nonetheless, stories past, present, and future have taken center stage in spiritual practices because of the ways they tell us about the

---

30. Joseph LeDoux, *The Emotional Brain: The Mysterious Underpinnings of Emotional Life* (New York: Touchstone, 1996), 275.

31. Antonio Damasio, *The Feeling of What Happens: Body and Emotion in the Making of Consciousness* (New York: Harcourt Brace, 1999), 287–89.

joys, fears, values, and commitments of the people we are and of the people for whom we offer care.

Attention to story frees us from a rigid diagnostic approach to assessment and care, one that tries to fit people into boxes. At the same time, story provides for us new possibilities in interpreting our stories in the context of God's story. Intersecting our stories with stories of faith is not a simple academic or analytic venture; it is instead an emerging commitment of the self. Since words by themselves are not sufficient transformers of our stories, we turn to an exploration of the role of action and performance — the role of ritual.

Chapter 4

LIVING AS IF...
Ritual, the Brain,
and Human Experience

Pulses keep unchanging phenomenon alive. This process of re-newing attention comes so naturally to us that our nervous systems add pulse where none is found.   —Robert Jourdain[1]

Ritual is not a word I have always been willing to use to describe what goes on in church. Ritual is not a category of activities I used to think of as conducive to healing or to right relationship with God. I grew up in a religious tradition that saw itself as determinedly non-ritualistic, or even antiritualistic. We left that to the Catholics and the Episcopalians. We saw ritual as hollow and empty, as repetitive recitations from people who read or quoted from rote memory, paying little attention to the meaning of the words. Seldom if ever were people really affected or changed by what happened in these ritual practices, as far as we could tell. Our pastors would never have thought about using a sermon manuscript. During my early years my home church even refused to print a worship bulletin, preferring to leave the order of service to the Holy Spirit. Needless to say, we seldom recited the creeds of the church, though we did follow a prepared order for the Lord's Supper, and we were quite familiar with the Lord's Prayer.

Instead of long or written liturgies, though, we had a number of practices in that little church that, by hindsight, undoubtedly deserve

---

1. Robert Jourdain, *Music, the Brain, and Ecstasy: How Music Captures Our Imagination* (New York: Avon Books, 1997), 126.

116

the label of ritual. There was a definite pattern to the use of music and Bible reading, there were clear expectations about what we would do at particular times and places, and there was even a special language ("Amen" and "Praise the Lord" were common phrases) that we used in church. Our Sunday mornings were more regulated than other services of the week. We knew exactly what to do when we sang songs — we often knew which songs were coming next. We knew how to give our testimonies in a public meeting, and we knew what to say during Bible study. Although no one ever saw a written list of instructions for worship, and seldom did anyone ever tell us how to participate in the life of the church, somehow we learned, somehow we knew.

One particular ritual that brought home the meaning of ritual to me was the altar call, or the invitation. The practice is alive and well in other churches and other traditions than my current one. For some it is a sacred ritual — the scene of God's most intimate encounters with human beings and the arena for profound conversions of heart, mind, and soul. Because it is so familiar to some of us, and perhaps unknown to others, we'll look at it more closely. More to the point, the altar call serves as a practice that gives some structure to our search for a definition and, hopefully, to some guidelines for the use of ritual in other settings.

In the church of my youth, this ritual almost always took place at the end of the service, after the sermon, and every sermon was designed to heighten our awareness of our need for God's grace. Whether the sermon had appealed to the heart or to the mind, the words were geared toward motivating us to reflect on our personal relationships with God and to consider public acknowledgment of, and remedy for, any disruption in that relationship. We could always tell when the preacher was making the transition from sermon to invitation; we were invited to a quiet, reflective time of prayer accompanied by piano or organ music, and then the altar was pronounced "open." The long walk down the aisle to the front of the church could indeed be a long one, particularly if you sat in the back pew. It was almost always performed to the music of "Just As I Am." With each step, we knew the eyes of parents, friends, and God were on us, even if surreptitiously. By coming forward, we were admitting a void in the center of our beings or a sense of shame and condemnation that darkened some corner of our lives. Once we knelt at the altar, we would pray alone or with the help of others, and the pastor would continue to invite or plead with others in the church to come forward. When it seemed more people were not willing to make that public a confession of need (or of sin), the pastor would provide an alternative. He would ask the congregation to keep their heads bowed to ensure privacy, and while the music continued to play softly, he (and it was almost always a "he" in those days) would invite those with needs to silently raise their hands. Sometimes there was a gentle encouragement for the hand raisers to come forward as well, but usually they were permitted to stay in place.

Members of the congregation would quietly slip forward to pray with those who had come forward. The reasons to come forward were as varied as the people who walked those aisles. Most felt some sense of guilt or shame and a desire for God's forgiveness. Often persons would come forward for a once-in-a-lifetime conversion. Sometimes, they came forward for a deeper sense of God's presence in their lives. Others might come forward for the healing of some hurt or of some illness; still others would come forward to pray on someone else's behalf. Others of course may well have come forward for less noble reasons — attention, reassurance, or compliance. But we knew how it was supposed to go. There was always a time of prayer that would last until the seeker felt some completion — a process known as "praying through." That might have required a matter of minutes or in some cases longer. After a brief word of testimony by the seeker, there would be a time of community prayer and thanksgiving, followed by a dismissal.

Now if I had used the word "ritual" to describe that experience, my pastor or members of that congregation would have corrected me right away. Ritual, after all, was empty and scripted. We didn't write people's prayers out for them. We invited people to pray in their own words, under the direction of the Holy Spirit. We didn't make people cross themselves or genuflect, or use "smells and bells" in our services.

For some of us, altar calls could be intrusive and abusive. And when they were prompted by manipulative sermons that induced unnecessary shame and guilt, they were abusive. But at its best, the altar call could be a ritual of the highest order. Sometimes it provided sacred space for genuine encounters with God; it could prompt genuine repentance and turn lives around. The altar call also involved the whole community in spiritual care for, and guidance of, each other. So why were we so reluctant to speak of ritual?

One of the dilemmas is that we understood ritual in a very narrow sense. We identified it with the particular rituals of particular denominations. We thought of highly formal worship that seemed to us to allow very little active participation by members and almost no freedom of expression. So using the word "ritual" in my home church would have invited trouble.

By understanding the ritual nature of life, we are able to learn more about what worship is, about how God becomes present to us and more about how we structure life to be meaningful. We are learning more about how rituals in the church help bind us together and how they draw us closer to God. We are learning about how our Protestant Christian worship is like that of our Roman Catholic and Orthodox sisters and brothers, as well as how it is different. But most important for our current discussion, we may be able to reclaim and harness more effectively the power of ritual for the healing and transforming of people's lives. In the process, I believe we can find that the roles of worship, pastoral counseling, and other spiritual practices share some critical dimensions.

Rituals and Counseling

Rituals have been "discovered" in the last couple of decades. Men's groups, women's groups, and marriage and family therapists are among those who have been talking about spirituality and ritual and telling us of their power. In the 1980s, marriage and family therapist Peggy Papp wrote:

> One can only wonder why the mental health profession has only recently begun to tap the power of this immense and natural source of healing.... [R]ituals can be used in therapy not only to *comment* on the experience but to actually *change* it. Since rituals make use of the stuff that dreams are made of — symbolism, fantasy, myths, and metaphors, they address themselves to the most primitive and profound level of experience.[2]

Does it amuse you (or sadden you) as it does me to realize that some of the discoveries of today are treasures that the church has held and practiced for centuries? After all, ritual is something religious communities know a great deal about, and have for quite some time. One can't help but wonder why people have not turned to the church for some insight or guidance in these matters a long time ago. Or more sadly, perhaps we have not made use of our ritual sense or made it known as a resource to others.

Thanks to our increased awareness of cultural diversity and to the marriage and family therapists, women's groups, and men's groups we noted above, the notion of ritual is very visible now. We explore this intriguing phenomenon with two outcomes in mind. The first is to argue that rituals are critical to healing and transformation, including the settings of pastoral counseling and spiritual practices. We have historically listened to people's stories but paid little or no attention to the rituals in their lives, and many hurting persons have stories that cry out for ritual. The second hoped-for outcome is to encourage worship that engages participants at the point of their own need. Worship that fails to connect with the day-to-day experiences, the griefs and anxieties of participants, is doomed to failure. In our worship, we lead people in the ceremonies and rituals of our faith, not

2. Peggy Papp, in Onno van der Hart, *Rituals in Psychotherapy: Transition and Continuity* (New York: Irvington Publishers, 1983), vii.

always attending to the ways these practices can heal human hurts or in some cases inflict them.

Pastoral theologian Herbert Anderson and liturgical theologian Ed Foley in their book *Mighty Stories, Dangerous Rituals* have reminded us that our worship and pastoral care often suffer from complementary problems. In pastoral care, we often encounter stories that have no rituals — no ways to mark or acknowledge life's changes, no ways to bring people into new ways of being and living. Losses like divorce, sending a child off to college, or the death of a child can bring suffering into our lives in ways that defy words. Too often, suffering persons have no opportunities to ritualize these experiences.

On the other hand, many of the rituals in which we participate regularly have lost their connection with story. Too often, Sunday morning participation in the Lord's Supper, baptism, and even the structures of the worship service itself have become disconnected from the stories that give them meaning. Our rituals become empty or hollow when they lose their connection with the original stories that set them in context. But perhaps even more significantly, our rituals lose their meaning when they become disconnected from our own personal stories.

What Do Rituals Do?

Rituals occur at many levels of life. We most often think of the rituals of worship and of faith. But not all our rituals are religious. Many of our rituals belong to our families, neighborhoods, schools, legal system, or even our sports teams. Other rituals are private practices that structure our day, such as the order with which we complete tasks in preparation for leaving the house (though as we note below, rituals by definition are usually public). Most rituals have been developed over time as safe havens from the stress of life or ways to deal with life changes. Not all rituals accomplish the same purposes, and anthropologists and others who have attempted to define ritual have strikingly different definitions. In matters of ritual, it's often easier to describe what we're talking about than to offer precise definitions.

Let's offer a word first about what rituals do, what they seem to be good for, and why people keep asking for them and participating in them, even if they don't call them "rituals" per se. In their simplest sense, rituals *lift up an event and make it special.* They set the events of our lives apart as distinctive from the routine. Rituals single out something that is happening, or about to happen, and call our attention to it as notable and remarkable. "This is different. Pay attention; something important is going on here." Rituals are almost the emotional equivalent of a teacher saying, "This will be on the test." Our rituals make sure that significant events don't slip by us unnoticed.

Rituals also provide an *ordering* to our lives, both as individuals and as communities. They mark the transition points, like baptisms, retirements, weddings, or funerals. Rituals mark critical steps in the life cycle: transitions like birth, adulthood, marriage, and death. They also ground us in larger cycles, like the rhythms of the seasons and the passage of time. They thus remind us that we are part of a larger created order. In so doing, rituals can hold and sustain us and represent continuity even in the midst of change.

Rituals assist us in *moving* through life's painful losses as well as *deepening* our experience of our joys. Good rituals can help us move from one place to another in life. They can help us overcome the "stuckness" of experiences, attitudes, or circumstances that seem to hold onto us and keep us from moving ahead. They can be grounded in the deeply felt experiences of life or quietly reassure us of the familiar. Sometimes they remind us of important events in the past, like birthdays, wedding anniversaries, the Lord's Supper, or Easter.

But let's start with a definition to orient ourselves. I particularly like one written by therapist Onno van der Hart:

> Rituals are *prescribed symbolic acts* that must be *performed* in a certain way and in a certain order, and may or may not be accompanied by verbal formulas. Besides the formal aspects, an

experiential aspect of rituals can be distinguished. The ritual is performed with much involvement. If that is not the case, then we are talking about empty rituals. Certain rituals are *repeatedly* performed throughout the lives of those concerned; others, on the contrary, are performed only once (but can be performed again by other people).[3]

This is a rich definition, so let's use it to shape our discussion and think about the ways ritual is part of the healing and care we undertake as pastoral caregivers. The definition suggests at least four important dimensions of ritual: *prescription, symbol, performance,* and *repetition.* I add two other dimensions of ritual: its *public* nature and its *effectiveness.*

Prescribed

Good rituals are written out ahead of time. Though I use the word "written" metaphorically, at the very least we have an outline for what we do. In some cases, we have complete scripts. But in either case, rituals work because they have been planned and prepared for.

Our plans may be general or they may be specific, but there must be plans. We all knew how to behave in an altar call. There were no printed instructions. We learned from watching those around us. When the plan is an outline, there will be much flexibility about what can happen during the ritual. I might participate in an altar call to seek forgiveness for my sin, I might come for a deeper relationship with God, or I might be accepting God's call to ministry. The words I use are my own. They are not scripted for me. Other rituals require very precise behaviors, actions, words, or objects. They also determine who is permitted to participate and who is authorized to lead or administer the rituals. The Lord's Supper or eucharist is an example of such a ritual in many of our traditions. In short, our rituals may allow or even encourage self-expression, or they may emphasize

---

3. van der Hart, *Rituals in Psychotherapy,* 5–6; emphasis added.

precision and uniformity. We are all doing this in the same way at the same time. But in either case, there is still a plan.

But Prescribed by Whom? And When?

The plans for some rituals have a long history. The eucharist has centuries of history, as do baptism or Christian initiation. Other rituals have shorter histories, such as the altar call. The altar call was not developed by the pastor or members of my congregation. Instead it had deep historical roots in the frontier camp meeting movement among Methodists and Baptists during the settlement of the eastern and midwestern United States. It also had roots in the preaching of Puritans like Jonathan Edwards. Other rituals have still shorter histories. A family may plan a ritual for a once-in-a-lifetime event: to welcome home an alcoholic parent who is returning from extended treatment, to mark the transition of an aging parent to a nursing home, to celebrate getting one's driver's license or (often with mixed feelings) the departure for college of a firstborn child. But whether a ritual has a long or a brief history, there is a plan.

The very word "ritual" evokes for many a sense of history and tradition. Some even argue that "creating rituals" is an oxymoron. Rituals are received, either from God or from the accumulated wisdom of previous generations of the faithful who have worshiped God. Others contend that rituals are being constantly created. Even in the reenactment of ancient rituals, those rituals are being changed to meet the circumstances of the day. The only rituals that really work, they say, are those that we have discovered or created for ourselves. The truth is likely somewhere in between. Or better yet, there is truth in both positions.

We may create ritual plans for ourselves, but some of our most powerful rituals are those that others have created. Some of our rituals are meaningful because of their history. They are gifts to us much more than they are our own private creations. When we know that we are doing what our families, our church, or other citizens of our country have done for decades or even centuries before us, we have a sense of participating in the life of our generations. When we pray together the Lord's Prayer or sing a familiar hymn, we may feel ourselves surrounded by "so great a cloud of witnesses."

Prescription involves at least two steps — planning and preparation. *Planning* may well have been done by those who will participate in the ritual or by others for the participants (such as initiates), or plans may have been received from preceding generations. *Preparation,* on the other hand, speaks to the ways we get ready to participate in the actual ritual moment. Both participants and officiants may well have very prescribed preparations that become rituals in their own right, such as rites of purification. In many Christian traditions, preparation for participation in sacraments such as the eucharist includes confession or repentance. We don't just jump into worship, pastoral counseling, or other rituals without thinking. These activities place us in a sacred space. We must prepare before we can participate.

One of the central outcomes of preparation is *anticipation.* Because rituals set apart time and space as distinctive, as time and space like no other, they inevitably focus our attention on what is to come. Preparation heightens participants' growing awareness that what is coming will matter in ways that few other events do. In some cases those rituals will even be life-changing. Whether they involve looking forward to a graduation ceremony, senior prom, wedding, or birthday dinner at a favorite restaurant, anticipation is often more than half the fun.

Of course anticipation of rituals is not always fun, just as rituals are not inevitably occasions of great happiness. Even the most joyful of celebrations can bring painful or at least uncomfortable feelings. Weddings and graduations, two of the most happily anticipated rituals of life, also represent loss — the loss of singleness, the loss of familiar lives with good friends. And the most sorrowful of ceremonies, such as funerals, can also elicit feelings of gratitude. Rituals in fact are containers for mixed feelings. We bring to them our feelings of love and hate, of fear and peace, of sorrow and joy. Ritual space at its best provides a safe setting for the experience of conflicting feelings.[4] It is likely that the heightened attention to gesture, feeling, and thought that are characteristic of ritual make available to us the deep ambivalence we feel about much in life. Perhaps the nervousness we pastors have observed in bridegrooms before the wedding is as much a response to the self-consciousness of ritual as it is to a fear of public speaking or of forgetting vows! Rituals by virtue of their structure invite anticipation, even among the most veteran participants.

Anatomy of a Ritual

Classical definitions of ritual have come to us primarily from the discipline of cultural anthropology. Scholars of other cultures have been particularly attentive to rituals and celebrations in those cultures because they understand rituals to be unique windows into the structures of the societies they want to know. Of particular interest to anthropologists have been rites of passage, those unique, once-in-a-lifetime intensive coming-of-age rituals that mark publicly and once and for all that this person is no longer a child in this society. From this point on, this person will be an adult among us.

The term "rites" refers to specific ritual practices that are broadly recognized within a community. They are concrete performances that a group has developed over time. While adolescent rites are the most familiar, there are many other passages that may be marked by particular ceremonies. Birth, death, and marriage are particular examples, and virtually all cultures have developed ritual ways to deal with these universal experiences. Death was likely the first passage for which human cultures developed careful ceremonies.[5] But it is the ways other cultures manage the transition from childhood to

---

4. Elaine Ramshaw, *Ritual and Pastoral Care* (Minneapolis: Fortress Press, 1987), 30–33.
5. Ronald L. Grimes, *Deeply into the Bone: Reinventing Rites of Passage* (Berkeley: University of California Press, 2000), 218–19.

adulthood that seems to have captured the interest of Western anthropologists, and has provided the most commonly accepted model of ritual structure.

More recently, ritual studies scholar Ronald L. Grimes has provided a noteworthy and helpful critique of this model.[6] First, rites of passage are not the only forms of ritual in which people engage. Rituals have varied purposes, and moving from one status in the culture to another is not the only one. Therefore, other models may well need to be developed and utilized in understanding the varieties of ritual's architecture. Second, as we noted above, coming-of-age rites are far from the only type of rites of passage. In addition to birth, marriage, and death, for instance, there are ceremonies of initiation into and out of other groups, and not all cultures practice rites of initiation. Third, rites of passage have focused primarily on the experiences of boys becoming men, with significantly less attention to rites of passage for women. So we must be cautious about relying on even the most commonly accepted ritual models.

With all those cautions in mind, we can safely use rites of initiation to examine the classical model of ritual and explore its relationship to worship and pastoral care. Anthropologist Arnold van Gennep is credited with first articulating the three-stage structure of rites of passage.[7] He observed in primitive cultures that rituals have (1) a preliminal (separation) phase, (2) a marginal or liminal phase, and (3) a postliminal (reincorporation) phase.

In the separation phase, initiates are physically removed from the communities in which they have been living as children. Often they are taken to a temporary encampment that has been constructed outside the village and to which no one other than the initiates and their elders are admitted. In other cases, they are taken into a nearby forest or field. The point of the movement is to remove the child from all the routines and structures that supported their identity as children. No

---

6. Ibid., 100–107.
7. Arnold van Gennep, *The Rites of Passage* (London and Henley: Routledge and Kegan Paul, 1960), 21.

longer do the cultural roles and rules apply. Children enter a strange new world in which they no longer know how to act. They must learn their way all over again. This condition in some ways represents a reenactment of the dependency experienced during infancy.

The liminal phase gets its name from the Latin word *limen*, meaning threshold. In a very real sense, children are stepping across a threshold from childhood to adulthood. In this marginal stage of rites of passage, the former-children-not-yet-adults are immersed in an unfamiliar and inevitably frightening period that may range from several days to several months. Employing a variety of methods, the elders engage in a deconstructionist pedagogy that is designed to help initiates leave behind their former roles and self-understandings. Children may be left on their own to find their own food and shelter, subjected to evil spirits in the form of masked dancers, or forced to face physical trials. In some cultures, deconstruction is followed by a reconstruction period in which they are taught the ways of adults. To make the critical transition from one life stage to another, one must dramatically, forcefully, and sometimes painfully leave behind former ways of being, earlier ways of experiencing oneself. To be transformed, one must live with an extended period of deep uncertainty.

The final step of the process is the reincorporation stage. Now the former children return to their communities as adults. They enter a new stage of learning and formation in which they live into the new roles for which they have been preparing. From now on, they have the responsibilities and privileges of fully functioning members of the society. The process is never complete without reentry into the community from which they have come. Adulthood must be experienced firsthand for new roles and understandings to be fully embodied, both for the new adults and for the community of which they are a part.

So Your Point Would Be...?

Even if van Gennep's model is not a pure fit for all rituals, there are clear echoes of our own experience in his outline. Some of the similarities between worship and pastoral counseling become evident: For ritual to be effective, we must separate ourselves from the rhythm of everyday life. We may slow down, or we may speed up, but we must step out of the way things are and step into a time and space that we experience as distinctly different. The boundary between daily living and the sacredness of the ritual time is clearly marked so that neither can be mistaken for the other. In worship, we generally make this transition through a prelude, a "time of gathering," an invocation. In private devotional practice, such as preparing to meditate or pray at home, we may listen to music, light a candle, read a devotion or Bible passage, or attend to our breathing. In counseling and spiritual direction, we invite clients into a room that is set apart at an appointed time. We develop rituals of greeting and rituals of opening that mark the session as beginning. Rituals may not be as evident in other pastoral care encounters, such as a visit to a patient in the hospital. Yet the offering of prayer or the simple fact that it's the pastor who is visiting may mark the time as distinct from routine or ordinary time. As the pastor represents the church, the congregation, or God, her or his walking into the room may in fact serve to change the meaning of the moments of the visit.

In all these settings, we generally imagine that the real work takes place in between the separation and the reincorporation phases, at a time when the rules and expectations are different. The demands and responses that typify most of life are suspended and a new way of relating to self, to others, and to God is enacted. It is a period in which we can live "as if" God's kin-dom is present now.[8] It is a time in which grace may truly abound, when we can safely "speak the truth in love" (Eph. 4:15), when relatedness and honesty and exploration can characterize our very being — in ways not possible in the daily course of life. We pass the peace and confess our failures in anticipation of forgiveness; with a trusted counselor, we voice hidden strengths that

---

8. The increasingly used word "kin-dom" is utilized here to emphasize the connectional, relational nature of God's presence rather than the hierarchical, patriarchical connotations of the more familiar "kingdom."

we fear would drive away the people on whom we depend; we speak of a presence behind the ups and downs of daily living that might lead others to label us as "crazy" or as religious fanatics. In ritual settings we welcome the hidden aspects of ourselves and our communities. We return later to this notion of "living as if...."

An often overlooked phase of both counseling and worship is the *reincorporation* phase. Living in a time and space apart from the routine requires a time and movement back to "the way things usually are." We required preparation to enter this separate space and time, and it requires just as intentional a return. We need to prepare ourselves (and our worshipers, clients, and ourselves) for the world and the way it usually works. In worship, our closing hymn, charge, benediction, and postlude signal the boundary of reincorporation. "Go out into the world to serve" marks a transition for many. In spiritual practices at home, an alarm clock, knock at the door, or telephone ringing too often signals the end of meditation or prayer time. In counseling sessions all too often the words "I'm sorry, our time is up" serve a similar function. Attentive counselors intentionally or intuitively sense the approaching end of an encounter and begin the process of "reentry" in ways that are much less abrupt. If the rituals of counseling, spiritual practice, and worship are to be truly safe places for encounter and transformation, we need to attend equally to entry and departure from these sacred times.

So far so good. Our altar call fills the bill as a ritual. There is a plan, even if it is a plan that allows for significant variation and self-expression. There is a time of preparation, of singing, of preaching. And this particular ritual brings with it a long history of practice and meaning that provide the overall structure for individuals who bring their own personal or private meanings to it.

Symbolic rituals point to a reality beyond themselves. They are signposts rather than destinations. The full meaning and power of rituals are never contained in the actions or objects of the ritual alone. They are instruments or pathways to a deeper understanding of unseen or spiritual realities. When I shake hands with someone, I am not just making physical contact. I am communicating friendliness, or at least saying that I don't plan to hurt anybody. When I exchanged rings with my wife during our wedding, I was doing much more than saying, "I think you'd look good in this." When we partake of communion we are feeding much more than our physical bodies — there's hardly enough nutrition to sustain us for very long.

We live in breathing bodies and in a world of things we can see, touch, smell, taste, and hear. Yet touchable, visible objects can also connect us to the spiritual and unseen realities of which we are not usually aware.

Words are symbols. They represent something other than themselves. They point to particular objects, people, places, or ideas. However, I am using the word "symbolic" in a different and tentative way here, because symbols and words share important characteristics. For the sake of illustration, I am drawing a stronger distinction than is generally warranted.

A primary value of words is their *precision*. The more we trust that a word means just one thing — at least in a particular context — the more it communicates to us, at least in a technical sense. Language commonly works to exclude alternate meanings so that we can be sure we are picturing in our minds exactly what the speaker or writer has intended. This is not true of all language, however. Some language, such as poetry, jokes, or metaphors, depends on breaking open the meanings of words. But our common use of language makes use of its precision. When we want to understand exactly what someone means or be sure they understand us, we rely on carefully chosen words.

Symbols of the nonverbal kind, on the other hand, have multiple meanings. Remember the gifts of the right hemisphere — the ability to make multiple connections at once, to see the bigger picture? Nonverbal symbols rely more on connotation than on denotation. They are often intentionally ambiguous, even as they point unambiguously to the unseen. Different people discover different meanings in the same ritual. Some of us find different meanings at different times in the same ritual. And all of us find multiple levels of meaning as we participate in one ritual. The symbolic meaning changes as our needs change.

Ironically, when we try to make the meaning of particular rituals — let's say Holy Communion/eucharist — too precise, we do injustice to the very purpose of the ritual. Symbol and ritual, like the Holy Spirit, help us express those "sighs too deep for words" (Rom. 8:26). When we try to limit too severely what a symbol is allowed to mean, we kill its spiritual power. How often has the immense power of a ritual dissolved in our inadequate attempts to describe it in words! By their very nature, movements and objects as symbols communicate and support what words alone cannot. Not all human experiences require explanation or definition. Symbols work in ways that words cannot. A gesture, a touch, a kiss of peace, flowing water — all can touch us in ways that are beyond the reach of words. Once again, overreliance on the brain's left hemisphere's skills at analysis and ability to employ language can rob us of the right hemisphere's capacity for ambiguity and multiple meanings.

Here is where our understanding of memory and imagination helps. Remember how the right brain's function is to hold many meanings in mind at one time? It is the caretaker of the bigger picture, while the left brain handles the details. The left brain watches the clock while the right brain has no sense of time — time stands still on the right side of our brains. Our right brains have this uncanny ability to put things together in whole new ways, to see possibilities that our left brain can't begin to imagine. The left brain's interpreter, or the cognitive imperative that requires us to understand, is complemented by the right brain's capacity for symbol and mystery. To be sure, both left and right hemispheres need each other to work well, but the right brain is better at this symbol stuff, unbound by single meanings. It can create the possibilities that the left brain cannot see. Our right hemispheres likely enable us to see beyond what our senses present to us.

I am a lover of puns — often to a fault. Just ask anyone who has known me for more than a few hours. If a word can have two meanings, I pick a third or fourth and have some fun with it. This very capacity is directly related to the right brain's competition with the left brain's need to explain. When we can understand that a situation means something very different from what it looks like, we are stretching our imaginations, we are seeing the unseen, we are being truly sacramental.

How is our altar call holding up? Surely the acts of walking, kneeling, and praying point to something beyond themselves. These actions communicate at their best a sense of remorse and contrition, of repentance and confession. And the community gathered around a seeker in prayer will for many embody the presence of Christ. They suggest the presence of a listening God and offer promise of an unseen (but believed) forgiveness. Surely this is a symbolic act.

Performed

Until a ritual is enacted, it does not exist and it serves no personal or community function. Reading about a ritual is not the same as participating in it. Until we go through the prescribed symbolic actions of the ritual, we have no experience of the ritual or of the grace it makes available to us. While there may be other avenues to grace, acting on our faith brings it home.

Faith and wholeness are *embodied* experiences. We cannot relegate them to the mind/brain or even to the spirit alone. They are grounded in our physical bodies as well. Our thoughts and feelings, our memories and imagination have their homes in neurons, muscles, and bones. Evidence has mounted dramatically in recent decades that our minds and our bodies truly belong to each other. When one gets sick, the other is at risk. When one gets well, the other benefits.[9]

---

9. See, for example, Harold G. Koenig, Michael E. McCullough, and David B. Larson, *Handbook of Religion and Health* (New York: Oxford University Press, 2001); Herbert Benson

To think of spirit apart from body, and body from spirit, is getting harder and harder. They are woven tightly together to such a degree that, if we attempt to keep our bodies out of our spiritual practice, our spirits suffer. Some of our religious traditions do better than others at involving the body and the senses in worship and pastoral care. Worship that invites or prescribes physical movement and extravagant visual imagery provides opportunities for immersion in the symbolic activity of ritual. Rather than viewing the body as a distraction from the things of the spirit, sensory-rich worship comprehends the body as a path to spirit.

Life, vitality, and spirit are grounded in our bodies. In fact, through our bodies we touch, taste, and feel in ways that form the basis for our experiences of God. While we are often reminded of the different facets of self, body, mind, and spirit, more often we neglect their deep interconnectedness. There is a reason that Paul said "Do you not know that your bodies are members of Christ?" (1 Cor. 6:15). While he was arguing for self-discipline and appropriate sexual expression, his words remind us today that our physical beings are the home for our deepest encounters with God. In fact, the Bible is replete with sensuous physical images of our relationship with God. "Taste and see that the Lord is good" (Ps. 34:8). "Hear O Israel, The Lord is our God, the Lord alone" (Deut. 6:4). "How sweet are your words to my taste, sweeter than honey to my mouth!" (Ps. 119:103). "They shall again live beneath my shadow, they shall flourish as a garden; they shall blossom like the vine, their fragrance shall be like the wine of Lebanon" (Hos. 14:7). The point is this: our spirits need our bodies as much as our bodies need our spirits. Full spirituality immerses us body, mind, and spirit in the life of God who breathed into our bodies the breath of life.

What would it mean for our worship if we were to find ways that people could bring their bodies with them! Do we invite people to move and act, or do we demand that they sit quietly and listen? What

---

with Marg Stark, *Timeless Healing: The Power and Biology of Belief* (New York: Scribner, 1996).

ways do we have for people to enact the stories we are telling in worship? What ways do we have for people to enact the stories they are telling us in pastoral counseling? Words are surely not enough. We need to find ways for people to perform their faith.

Our altar call example is still doing OK. It is an act that must be carried out, steps that must be taken. When freely chosen, it gives us opportunity to live out the experience of confession and repentance. I am reminded of a congregation I served that celebrated the Lord's Supper the first Sunday of the month. At the end of that service, all present would form a circle around the perimeter of the sanctuary, hold hands, and sing "Blest Be the Tie That Binds." In this simple ritual, they too put flesh on their words.

Repetition

Our fourth dimension, repetition, is optional. We often identify particular acts as rituals because we do them repeatedly. Some of our rituals, of course, are repeated over and over again so we can strengthen our memories and rehearse our stories. Our discussion in chapter 2 about the role of memory and rehearsal is important here. In repeating the stories and rituals of our lives and faith we reinforce their power and strengthen their role in our daily living. For those rituals that have been handed down to us from the past, our participation in them is a repetition of previous enactments. By involving myself in the Lord's Supper, for instance, I am living again not only the story of Jesus' last night with his disciples before his crucifixion. I am entering into the experience of millions of Christians all over the world who have gone before me.

We get familiar with our rituals and get comfortable participating in them. In fact, one of the benefits we get from our repeated rituals is a sense of reassurance that some things can stay the same. There can be discomfort the first time or two we participate in a ritual, particularly if it is a complex one. When my family and I worshiped one Easter in a high Episcopal church, I spent more time than I care to admit rehearsing the steps of taking communion — a step I never have to consider at my home church or at the seminary chapel. Rituals that are repeated remind us of the continuity of life. Not everything changes — some things stay the same.

Repetition and Memory

When we repeat rituals, we strengthen our memories of them. The rituals we practice throughout life can form a bedrock of memory even deeper than the stories we tell. Rituals practiced throughout life may remain as emotional and spiritual resources even when our ability to remember events begins to fail. Even as stories fade from memory with the passing of years, the gestures, behaviors, and words we have rehearsed for years may endure. Middle-age parents, returning to church after a decade or more of absence, report that the familiar prayers, movements, and words of worship return, like the skills involved in riding a bicycle.

In chapter 2, we noted the important distinctions between episodic, semantic, and procedural memory. We reported the evidence that these different forms of memory employ different brain systems. Remembering how to do something is different from remembering a particular event or fact. In performing rituals, in participating in them, we more deeply encode our memories for them. Rituals reinforce and depend on procedural memory because rituals are performed. They don't depend solely on the memory of a particular story. In all likelihood, the brain systems responsible for procedural memory are among the last to be destroyed by some degenerative diseases. That may be the reason the patient otherwise unable to recall what she had for lunch will not miss a word or gesture in a complex but familiar religious ritual like the eucharist.

Some of our rituals are performed frequently, and others occur much less often. Ordinations, baptisms, confirmations, and similar rituals occur once in the course of a lifetime for individuals. Their frequency in a given congregation depends on the size and makeup of that community. In other settings, other rituals are one-time-only occasions: turning twenty-one parties, initiating ceremonies for fraternities or sororities, or coming-out parties. Other rituals are performed quite regularly, such as eucharist (at least in some traditions), prayers, and worship services. Outside the church, Fourth of July parades and Super Bowl parties have ritual dimensions. Some anthropologists have observed that across cultures, the more frequent the ritual, the less dramatic and elaborate it is. More elaborate ceremonies engage the emotional life of participants more fully and, as a result, contribute to clearer and more vivid memories. In cultures that do not have the advantages of printed texts to maintain communal memories, vivid and precise memories are critical. Nonliterate cultures intuitively comprehend the difference and make more vivid and memorable those celebrations that are less frequent.

Frequency of repetition has an impact on which type of memory is reinforced.[10] Frequent participation in a ritual or story makes it less likely that a participant will remember any specific ritual event. Instead, frequency blends multiple events into a single memory. So frequent rituals probably support semantic memory, memories of fact or of "they way things are." The less often we participate in a ritual, the more we are able to recall individual celebrations and the more vivid those memories are for us. Infrequent rituals more effectively reinforce episodic memory.

Once again, the altar call fills the bill. In many traditions, this practice occurs weekly and its outline is familiar. But it introduces an interesting note into the practice of ritual. The altar call took place often, but it was not expected that any one person would respond to every invitation. It was different from communion. Certainly persons could come more than once, if the need arose, but generally the effect of an altar call was expected to last for a while. The situation arose in another church I served. A man in his early forties suffered serious

10. Robert N. McCauley, "Ritual, Memory, and Emotion: Comparing Two Cognitive Hypotheses," in Jensine Andresen, ed., *Religion in Mind: Cognitive Perspectives on Religious Belief, Ritual, and Experience* (Cambridge: Cambridge University Press, 2001), 115–40.

developmental problems, and though he was able to work, he lived with his retired parents. Every time an invitation was offered to the congregation, he was one of the first to respond. It became clear that this experience was healing and sustaining for him, perhaps serving some of the same functions that regular confession provides in other traditions. But one could also sense a slight discomfort from others in the congregation about this man's use of the ritual. His regular participation may have threatened the meaning of the altar call as a "one time only" or at least infrequent rite. Generally, expectations for responding to an altar call fell somewhere between the regular participation of communion and the once-in-a-lifetime experience of baptism. People like this man can call attention to the meanings of rituals, even as they may appear to others to misuse or overuse them.

Special Purpose

Some rituals may be developed and performed just once for a unique purpose. Some of life's special events or transitions don't have opportunities for celebration or ritual readily available, either in our communities of faith or in the culture. We're not typically offered rituals for beginning kindergarten, though my editor Ulrike Guthrie tells the following story:

> Our youngest child, Emelia, just started Kindergarten this fall. To mark the occasion, we continued the German tradition with her that my parents had done with me thirty-six years ago: they met me at the school gate at the end of the first day, as parents do in Germany to this day, holding a large Schultute — basically a prettily decorated cardboard cone — or originally a cornucopia, filled with little gifts: school supplies, toys, candy, all kinds of treats to sweeten the day, and make it less traumatic and something to look forward to.

We do not have rituals for declaring an adolescent an adult or completing a manuscript on time. We don't have ready-made ways to ritualize a miscarriage, though some denominations have begun to develop liturgies for different types of loss. Neither the culture nor the church offers couples models to ritualize their move into the post–child rearing days — a time we have referred to elsewhere as "promising again."[11] We don't have rituals for moving an aging parent into a retirement home or for grieving the reality of infertility. For persons and families facing these and other crucial moments, help may most effectively call for families and caregivers together to design new rituals that will name the reality and point the way to the future. In other cases, existing rituals may be used in new ways for the same purposes.

Special care must be taken in designing rituals and so a few guidelines are in order.

First, whenever possible, all participants should be involved in planning a ritual. In working with families, for instance, a family meeting to discuss the purpose of the ritual, the timing, and the structure of the ritual prepares all participants and promotes a sense of ownership.

Second, rituals should be simple rather than complex. Rituals that are too complicated can lose focus and cause participants to feel anxious about carrying out their parts or roles properly. Selecting one event to be celebrated and one particular high moment in the ritual is most effective. Placement of the central actions of the ritual should be carefully considered. Placing a symbolic act too early in the ritual can make the rest of the ritual appear anticlimactic. Placing it at the end may fail to offer participants a time to prepare for reentry into postritual time and space. Students in a recent class, for instance, wrote and enacted a ritual for divorce. A sand tray held small clay figures representing each member of the family, arranged in a circle. A particularly powerful moment came when the divorcing parents moved their own figures away from each other, breaking the circle. Had the ceremony ended there, participants would have had no time

---

11. Herbert Anderson, David Hogue, and Marie McCarthy, *Promising Again* (Louisville: Westminster John Knox Press, 1995).

to live into the new reality. Had the facilitators included several ritual acts afterward, they would have diluted the richness of the moment. Timing matters.

Third, select words and actions that all participants can agree to. Many rituals, particularly those in the church or with large groups, become coercive when they require people to say or do things they have not considered or consented to. Ritual honesty is a requirement for effective use of rituals.[12] Asking children to declare their trust in divorcing parents when they've not yet experienced their new families asks too much; promising again to a spouse after an affair demands that the woundedness and injustice of the betrayal be acknowledged and addressed; even printed declarations in worship may ask worshipers to make commitments they cannot fully own.

Fourth, debriefing and evaluating the ritual at some time soon after the ritual has taken place extends the effectiveness of the ritual moment and enables the family or group to further develop its skills in ritualizing. Immediately revisiting the ritual has the advantage of freshness and clear memory. A day or two later might offer some perspective that only time would allow. At the same time, this group might make plans for doing rituals in the future.

Public

We think of rituals as public acts, performed with others who may participate at varying levels of involvement. The public nature of some rituals is what makes them powerful. In a class at the seminary, a colleague and I asked two students to design a ritual for divorce. The service was carefully and sensitively done, acknowledging that the congregation was called together not to celebrate a divorce, but to celebrate the steadfast presence of God in all of life's pains and joys.

The ritual was clearly a role-play — we all knew that. But that did not stop us from experiencing the pain as two actors declared

---

12. Ramshaw, *Ritual and Pastoral Care*, 26–28.

their singleness and returned rings to each other in a silent act. We watched, as a temporary congregation, as two "parents" vowed in front of these witnesses to continue to love and care for each of their "children" in turn. We watched this divorcing couple as they gave gifts to each child, symbols of the relationship they hoped to have with them. And everyone there participated in the rituals of blessing these two people as they went their separate ways. The two students who wrote the ritual found themselves deeply touched during its enactment and looked to the two of us professors for some reassurance. We were too busy reaching for tissues.

When rituals are performed in the presence of caring and committed witnesses, their power is multiplied. The old adage — joys shared are multiplied and sorrows shared are diminished — seems quite true. And if a role-played recognition of divorce can engage us all so powerfully — even when we know we are pretending — how much more powerfully do rituals of real life serve as containers for the deeper feelings of joy and pain that are their inevitable companions?

Some rituals take place more privately. Some events that prompt us to ritual are too sensitive to share the intimate details much beyond our families or ourselves. When a couple promises again after the end of one partner's affair, they may wish to name the wrongs and seek forgiveness within a smaller circle. Ritualizing an abortion or miscarriage may best be limited to those directly involved.[13]

But there is a danger here. North American individualism has so emphasized privacy and confidentiality that we lose the power and support of the communities to which we belong. Pastoral care and counseling have followed this trend from the early days of the last century. Pastoral theology broadened its focus of concern from individuals to families in the middle of the last century. And now in the last few decades we have reminded ourselves that the larger systems of church and community, of culture itself, influence the health and well-being of the persons we are called to serve, and vice versa.

---

13. Grimes, *Deeply into the Bone*, 315–20.

One of the consequences of our rediscovery of ritual is an effort to involve individuals more openly and deeply in the communities that shape our lives together. We know in ways we have not known before that we all need each other. We have been discovering the isolation and shallowness to life that result when we try to live lives totally unto ourselves. Rituals that welcome other people into the crises of life have a place in linking us together again. We probably need to learn again what it means to be the body of Christ.

Effective

When most of us think of rituals, we think of ceremonies that mark something that has already happened or is taking place with or without the ritual itself. Those events will have happened and have their effects on our lives whether or not we ritualize them. They are simply calling attention to that which is. They are remembrances. A friend recently told me she doesn't like to have birthday parties. She's convinced herself that if she doesn't celebrate a birthday, she will not age!

Some rituals actually bring about the changes they are also observing. Weddings, for instance, at least in the eyes of the church, have been understood to join a couple together in the presence of God. Before the wedding, the participants are two separate people. Afterwards they are a couple.[14] For some of us, our ordination services turned us from laypersons into clergypersons. In the moments a president is inaugurated, he or she stops being president-elect and becomes president. Without the performance of some rituals, the changes they celebrate don't occur.

Most of our rituals aren't like that. But by the same token, when rituals really work, they *are* bringing about change in the very process of performing them. Theologian Tom Driver distinguishes, helpfully,

---

14. Herbert Anderson and Robert Cotton Fite, *Becoming Married* (Louisville: Westminster John Knox Press, 1993), 112–37.

between Shelter rituals and Pathway rituals.[15] Shelter rituals are those rituals that sustain us in times of distress or change. They underscore the continuity of life. Communion is a good example, as are our celebrations of the seasons and national historic remembrances like Independence Day. Pathway rituals help us move from one condition or status to another. They ease transitions that otherwise would be invisible or severely painful. Baptisms and funerals are good examples here.

For instance, our culture has not offered much in the way of rites of passage for teenagers, as we have already noted. A child physically matures, becomes capable of adult acts, and even develops more advanced cognitive skills whether we celebrate the change or not. But other dimensions of adulthood do not take place until rites of passage have occurred. In some cultures, for instance, without undergoing the often-treacherous rituals of adulthood, a young man or woman would continue to be a child in the eyes of the society. Whether a child has reached physical maturity or not, her or his recognized adulthood is not real until it has been celebrated. There are many reasons for the difficulties our children experience growing up in this culture. But perhaps part of that difficulty lies in the fact that it is hard to know when in fact we are adults.

Precious few rituals in our culture make real the transition from childhood to adulthood. In most of our churches, confirmation or baptism has been the rite of choice, somewhat parallel to the Jewish celebrations of bat and bar mitzvah. But few churches make enough of a point of these rituals to ensure that they will be meaningful, or even that they will become anything more than an additional graduation ceremony. In all likelihood, getting a driver's license and high school graduation are the cultural rituals available to us. Possibly the intensely ritualized character of gang membership has been a response in part to this need for marking our transitions from childhood to adulthood. Perhaps this is one of many opportunities for the church

15. Tom Driver, *The Magic of Ritual: Our Need for Liberating Rites That Transform Our Lives and Our Communities* (New York: HarperCollins, 1991), 71.

to respond with rituals that will aid in reclaiming the church's role in the lives of those we serve.

A student described to me a ritual at one congregation that celebrates the driver's license rite of passage. During morning worship, the recently licensed driver is welcomed to the front of the sanctuary where the pastor ceremoniously hands over a new set of car keys. In front of parents, congregation, and God, the new driver's accomplishment is celebrated, and the monumental responsibilities of driving are recalled. The whole community becomes part of this recognition and, similar to what occurs in baptism, begins to own its responsibility to the continuing nurture and guidance of this mobile Christian.

What's Happening Here?

So what is it that takes place in rituals that makes them such powerful transformers and healers? How can we understand this process better so we can make appropriate use of rituals in helping people grow and relate to God? We've already mentioned some features of ritual that help set certain times apart, heighten our expectancy for those times, and involve the broader community in marking transitions. But two more angles on this matter can broaden our understanding. We look first at the relationship between story and ritual and then return briefly to some relevant neuroscience discoveries.

Stories and experience come together in the rituals we enact. In communion the stories of Jesus' last night before his crucifixion are told in word and in ceremony. But the relationship between story, ritual, and experience is a complex one. We commonly think of rituals as enactments of stories. Rituals start with the stories we tell that are then expressed dramatically. We might diagram this one-way process like this:

Story → Ritual → Experience

Stories that shape who we are — biblical stories and other stories of faith — are then reenacted in rituals that in turn produce experiences of similar thoughts and feelings in us. These rituals draw us into the experiences of those who first told these stories, and perhaps even into the stories themselves.

Our rituals are rehearsals of the stories that define us. They remind us of who we are by allowing us to participate again in those events that are given to us in our history as the people of God. Here again we are reminded of the memory studies in chapter 2 where we noted that memories are most readily recalled when the emotional context in which they were experienced is re-created. By re-creating a context similar to that of early Christians, or of people in the biblical stories, we are enabled to re-member those stories more powerfully.

Theologian John E. Burkhart speaks helpfully of worship as rehearsal:

> Responsible worship *rehearses* graced reality.... Since God's will gives movement and pattern to reality, shaping history to its redemptive goal, worship takes on the dimension of rehearsal. It serves God by shaping and reshaping human lives to express what life is all about.[16]

If we return briefly to our understanding of the brain and of imagination, we remember those images and stories stored in the cortex. In ritual, those images are recalled and influence the feelings and bodily sensations in lower brain areas. Hence, from a neuropsychological perspective, we have a top-down approach to the relationship between story and ritual, moving from the cortex through lower brain regions and finally to the body itself. Both our left and right hemispheres reimage the stories we are told and then spread the news of those stories throughout our bodies. The brain treats imagination and memory in the same basic ways it does perception (chapter 1), including communicating through the body's hormonal and autonomic nervous systems. So when we enter into stories, the body responds as though it were actually there.

---

16. John E. Burkhart, *Worship: A Searching Examination of the Liturgical Experience* (Philadelphia: Westminster Press, 1982), 31.

While the enactment of stories is often an accurate description of ritual performance, there is a second way to understand the relationship between story and ritual. Our rituals may also grow out of our experience and then shape the stories we tell. This might be called a bottom-up approach. We could diagram it this way:

Experience → Ritual → Story

At first glance this process is counterintuitive. Yet our brains are resourceful organs, and they often prompt us to actions when we are not conscious of the cause. We take some actions just because they seem right. Eventually that interpreter in the left brain must make sense of what we are doing, and so a story is born. Like Roger Sperry's split-brain patients recalled in chapter 2, we write stories to make sense of the behaviors we observe in ourselves!

Driver suggests that the eucharist developed in this way.[17] He recalls the Emmaus Road story (Luke 24:13–35) in which Cleopas and an unnamed disciple meet the post-Easter Christ on their way home. They are troubled and confused, and they do not recognize Jesus. They share stories of what had happened, and the stranger reminds them of stories of Jesus. But not until they break bread together in Emmaus do they recognize him. Driver suggests that this story describes the early church's experience of breaking bread together. When they participated in the common meal, it seemed to them as though Jesus were there in their midst. To explain this novel but increasingly familiar experience, they then remembered and retold Jesus' words on the night of his arrest. That is, the experience of Jesus' presence called to mind the remembered sayings and actions of Jesus *in the event of reenacting the ritual.* What is key in this account is the possibility that story was recalled to explain the experience early Christians had of Jesus' continuing presence.

Some of our rituals may emerge even before the stories that explain them. Because of our need for meaning, we then search for (or create)

---

17. Driver, *The Magic of Ritual,* 210.

the stories that can give them meaning. Such an explanation is in line with what we know about the brain and particularly the role of the interpreter housed in the left hemisphere (see chapter 3).

There is at least a third understanding of the relationship between ritual and story. This relationship might be diagrammed as follows:

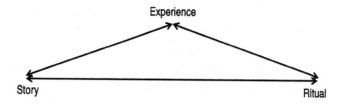

This diagram is truer to our experience. Both the top-down and the bottom-up approaches are included, as the ongoing, dynamic relationship between ritual, story, and experience is fleshed out. The relationships between them are no longer unidirectional. Story and ritual both must engage our experience for us to enter most fully into the life of faith. Our experiences energize the stories that our faith offers to us, and our faith provides order and meaning to the experiences that we encounter.

During the routine of the day, our brains depend most heavily on the dominant hemisphere, usually the left one in right-handed people. This is not surprising since much of everyday existence requires logic and problem-solving and calls on our use of language and sense of time. In ritual experience, on the other hand, we can experience just the opposite — a sense of timelessness and wholeness, which is more characteristic of the inferior (right-brain) hemisphere's activity. Participating fully in a worship service or other moment of ritual transcendence, therefore, likely involves both hemispheres of the brain. As we understand the words of the stories, as we follow the sequence and plot, we also notice a sense of timelessness and connection with those around us. Worship at its best — and pastoral care at its most effective — mirrors the wholeness of the self in the wholeness of the brain.

Ritual and the Brain

Some of the most intriguing research exploring ritual from the perspective of the brain has been emerging in an interdisciplinary enterprise linking the brain and cognitive sciences with cultural anthropology and religious studies. Advances in the technology of brain studies have enabled researchers to study the living, active brains of persons involved in a wide range of tasks, including meditation.[18] This is a significantly better approach than studying people's behavior and then waiting for them to die so an autopsy can be performed! What is emerging is a description of the brain at work during certain types of religious experience. Summarizing those findings in a few brief paragraphs would do the studies severe disservice. In addition, the exploration of the neurobiological processes underlying religious experience is still quite young and has not yet attracted the interest of neuroscientists widely enough to develop a credible framework or consensus about the exact processes involved. A third problem is that workable definitions of religious experience can be elusive.[19] As we have argued above, religious experiences rely on the same neuronal processes as other cognitive and emotional experiences.

Nevertheless, a couple of promising avenues of exploration appear to have particular relevance for ritual experience. First, the experiences that confront us daily are continuous — few if any natural "breaks" occur in the flow of information that bombards us from moment to moment. Yet the brain naturally and automatically divides those continuous experiences into discrete segments, as though it were dividing unbroken text into chapters and verses.[20] In a manner similar to the way the brain's visual system looks for the edges of objects, the brain seeks the edges of events, dividing them into

---

18. See, for instance, Eugene d'Aquili and Andrew B. Newberg, *The Mystical Mind: Probing the Biology of Religious Experience* (Fortress Press, 1999); Andrew Newberg, Eugene d'Aquili, and Vince Rause, *Why God Won't Go Away: Brain Science and the Biology of Belief* (New York: Ballantine, 2001).

19. Andresen, in Andresen, ed., *Religion in Mind*, 277.

20. Jeffrey M. Zack et al., "Human Brain Activity Time-Locked to Perceptual Event Boundaries," *Nature Neuroscience* 4, no. 6 (June 2001).

both larger and smaller segments. The brain automatically assigns beginnings and endings to the segments of observed events. Because the brain also selects particular objects out of the vast array in the environment at any one time, it assigns significance, or what psychologists call *salience,* to particular objects. It does not seem like much of a stretch to suggest that the brain may also see particular events or segments of events as standing out from others in terms of their importance. So the marking of the edges of ritual experience likely supports and mimics the brain's own processes in marking time.

Second, we have already spoken about some of the body's mechanisms to arouse itself (for instance, in a threatening situation) or to calm itself after the threat has passed (see chapter 1). Persons of faith who have truly been engaged in worship confirm that worship at its best (or even at its worst) evokes strong emotions, whether those feelings are joy, fear, peace, anger, or boredom. We recognize the experiences of arousal and of quiet. Psychiatrists Eugene d'Aquili and Andrew Newberg have modeled ways the arousal (sympathetic) and quiescent (parasympathetic) systems of the brain are engaged in ritual experiences, underscoring the ways those experiences are grounded in and expressions of the autonomic nervous system of the body.[21]

They suggest, not surprisingly, that slow rhythms in worship quiet us, and faster rhythms arouse us. Worship, they contend, should find a balance of both. That is nothing we didn't know already. But they also argue that, if we stimulate one system or the other (arousal or quiescent) far enough, eventually the other system also becomes activated, leading to the resonating vibrations of both hemispheres, a result they refer to as *spillover.* Such a state leads to an experience of ecstasy and connection with others around us. We readily observe these responses in charismatic congregations where speaking in tongues and other ecstatic utterances punctuate worship or in the repetitive praise choruses of many evangelical congregations.

---

21. d'Aquili and Newberg, *The Mystical Mind,* 99–108.

But more reserved worship settings can also produce a sense of transcendence and connectedness with fellow congregants. Followed even further, this condition can lead ultimately to a state d'Aquili and Newberg refer to as Absolute Unitary Being (AUB), which they claim is the goal of all of the world's major religions. Members of Western religious groups like Christianity will recognize the broad outlines of contemplation and mystical experience.

Meditation and ritual lead to the same end (merger with the divine, or AUB) but by different paths. Meditation is a top-down approach, beginning with the images in the brain which then influence brain and body responses through the limbic system and ultimately the brain stem. Ritual, by contrast, is a bottom-up experience in which participants physically experience fast or slow rhythms that follow a path from the body to the higher cognitive functions (except speech). Meditation requires much more practice and experience than ritual participation, but d'Aquili and Newberg believe that corporate ritual can lead to similar alternative states of consciousness.

These scholars attribute an important dimension of this experience to a part of the brain known as the left posterior superior parietal lobe, that is, the section of the parietal lobe that is near the top and back of the parietal lobe. This part of the brain, they argue, helps us recognize the separation between self and others — what we think of as our personal boundaries.[22] (Note the discussion of the neuropsychology of empathy in chapter 1.) They believe this function of the brain evolved from the brain's early ability to distinguish between objects that are graspable and those that are beyond reach — an important distinction for our early ancestors in search of food and tools. During ritual or meditation, input into that area of the brain decreases, resulting in a breakdown of the sense of separation between self and others. Our experience of connectedness with others, including God — of belonging — shows up in our brains as well. We might,

22. Ibid., 112.

in fact, think of worship as an experience of extended empathy as suggested in chapter 3.

At the same time, d'Aquili and Newberg argue, the parallel section of the right cortex is responsible for locating ourselves in space and time. The input to those sections of the brain is likewise inhibited (deafferented), resulting in a sense of timelessness and unlimited space. While criticized on the basis of limited empirical evidence, the theory clearly suggests important areas for further research.

While these conclusions will benefit from further exploration, the description of brain function as a platform for our experiences of God is convincing. The findings are also consistent with a central argument of this book: that our religious experiences make use of the processes and structures in the brain that are the same processes the brain employs in the daily activities of living and relating.

Living as If...

Whether we serve in worship, a pastoral counselor's office, the hospital, or small groups in the parish, we are shaping ritual time and ritual space, or if you prefer, sacred time and sacred space. We are speaking of those times of elevated expectancy, of deepened vulnerability, of a sense of profound connection with others and with the sacred that mark our encounters with God.

A central dimension of those ritual experiences is embodied in the experience of living, for a time, as though the world we imagine is really here. We use the phrase "virtual reality" to describes "worlds" constructed when information is presented to our senses that the unaided world does not offer. Those worlds can be changed at the will of the operator and take us places that have no existence apart from their images, or that we might never reach even if they did. Yet we live in them as though our bodies were right there. If you have any doubts about their "reality," spend time with a friend prone to motion sickness as she watches a movie of a car speeding down a winding San Francisco street. Or observe the faces of listeners transported by a performance of Randall Thompson's choral masterpiece "Peaceable Kingdom." Whether created by video cameras, computers, musicians, or worship facilitators, we live in virtual reality for a time. In ritual we are able to live in a world we can only imagine, but it is a world that we somehow know lies beneath the world of daily routine. In ritual, we suspend the "rules" that order our lives, but only for a time. It is a reality that we are not able to live in all the time; we need only glimpse it periodically to be reminded of its existence.

Living "as if" could suggest a kind of escapism, a vacation from the stresses and strains of daily living. And yet effective worship, like effective psychotherapy, offers a different possibility. When we live as if another reality were present in the world, we are changed. We do not return to the world quite the same. Liturgical scholar John Burkhart says it this way: "Worship changes humans. It honors God and helps humans; and because God's character is to share, the two are somehow interrelated."[23] We return to the world as different people when we have entered into a different time and lived as if the kin-dom of heaven were truly at hand. Those liminal experiences of encounter with another world are embodied in the practices of the church to which we turn at long last.

---

23. Burkhart, *Worship,* 32.

Chapter 5

WHAT THEN?...
The Practice of Pastoral Counseling

Quite simply, soul expresses meaning, and the making of mean-
ing depends on memory. To mind the soul is to attend to
meaning making. — James B. Ashbrook[1]

Brain, imagination, memory, story, and ritual. We've covered much territory in the first four chapters, hinting at some of the implications for practices of the church. We've spoken of different spiritual practices almost interchangeably. In chapters 5 and 6, we look at pastoral counseling, worship, and spiritual disciplines in turn, considering the roles the brain and ritual play in understanding and implementing those practices. Following two brief caveats about our venture, we consider further the soul, trajectory, and ritual, turning next to spiritual practices, considering the distinctive ways each nurtures the soul.

Pastoral counseling, worship, and spiritual practices constitute only part of the church's activities. Nonetheless, they are activities characterized to varying degrees by their ritual nature, by the ways they set time apart from the ordinary, and by their twofold purposes of sustaining and transforming those who participate in them.

Pastoral counseling, a specialized form of the broader historical category of pastoral care, is distinguished by its focus on particular identified problems in living and an agreement for regular, generally

---

1. James B. Ashbrook, *Minding the Soul: Pastoral Counseling as Remembering* (Minneapolis: Fortress Press, 1996), 170.

time-limited meetings. Pastoral counseling emphasizes privacy and confidentiality. While other forms of pastoral care may be offered in a variety of settings, pastoral counseling is generally offered in locations apart from the public life of a congregation or institution — a pastor's office or counseling room, a counseling center or private office.[2]

Worship describes religious communities gathered for (usually) public rituals. Worship is generally the center of a congregation's religious life, offering prayer, praise, petition, and frequently preaching. In most Christian traditions, worship involves the celebration of sacraments, unique rituals understood to express the heart of the church's identity.

Spiritual practices include a wide range of activities, including not only public worship, but also prayer, small groups such as covenant or Bible study groups, and individual or group spiritual direction. They are practiced by individuals, groups (including families), and congregations.

Giving away a punch line at the beginning of a joke nearly always destroys the surprise of the joke. So does telling the end of the story to a movie watcher. Reading a text that attempts to cover as many topics as this one does, however, may actually be enhanced by knowing the outcome. So in brief, here is where we are headed: Our most transformative religious practices are liminal experiences — boundaried periods of time in which routine is left behind, norms and rules are suspended, and we experience life as if it were some other way. Memory and imagination locate us in history by telling and hearing stories of past, present, and future. Paradoxically, rituals also lift us beyond time. They transform by transporting us to worlds that are yet to be and returning us to our everyday worlds as new creations. The more deeply we realize and enact the ritual nature of spiritual practice, the more we are open to the uniquely sacred. We experience

---

2. Rodney J. Hunter, "Pastoral Care and Counseling," in Rodney J. Hunter, ed., *Dictionary of Pastoral Care and Counseling* (Nashville: Abingdon Press, 1990), 845.

life the way it could be, or should be, if the presence of God were more fully recognized and welcomed in the world.

On Science and Practice

In these final chapters we are walking a tightrope. The fascinating discoveries of the brain sciences over the last several decades have too often led to marked excesses of speculation about what those discoveries mean for good practice in areas as diverse as art, music, creativity, mathematics, psychological disorders, and religion. Claims have been made that far exceed what the science will support.

Too much caution about application carries other risks. Because science is an ongoing process, we could wait much too long to reap the benefits of recent discoveries. But more important, we would miss a critical opportunity as practical theologians to be involved in asking questions of scientists as they do their work. We could lose our opportunity to participate in shaping the questions that science is investing untold energy and resources into answering. So in this volume we are attempting to balance caution with the risks of speculation. Those speculations are always subject to further research and testing in action.

A Matter of Ethics

Likewise, though less dramatically, the field of ritual studies, grounded in the methods of anthropology, has become a significant resource for religious leaders. Our increasing awareness of the religious pluralism in our neighborhoods as well as in our world has confronted us with the tangible reality of the richly varied ways peoples of the world worship. As discussed in chapter 4, many have experienced a poverty of rituals in our highly industrialized Western culture. The increasing visibility of ritual practices around the world (particularly rites of passage) has created an intense interest bordering on nostalgia or even voyeurism. Many are "borrowing" ritual practices from cultures that are not their own. One-time participants frequently know little about the meanings of a ritual, let alone about the broader cultural implications and histories of which these rituals are a part. Such practices border on "ritual cannibalism."

In seeking to quench our thirst for rituals, it is critical to remember that stories and rituals are part and parcel of the cultures which gave them birth. When we consider borrowing or participating in those rituals, we need to acknowledge and adhere to several ethical guidelines. First, we should be particularly certain that members of those groups or societies whose rituals we want to experience truly welcome us and invite our participation. Some Native American groups, for instance, have said they deeply resent Caucasian Americans who have intruded on sacred ceremonies with lack of respect for the people and/or for the meaning of the rituals they were conducting. Those who wish to experience rituals from other cultures, therefore, should be clear and honest about their intentions and be sure potential hosts have the right to decline.

Second, people who consider participating in other cultural rituals owe it to themselves and to their hosts to be well informed ahead of time about the meaning and details of the rituals they will observe or participate in. Becoming well informed is not an easy or haphazard endeavor. It requires careful preparation, often including reading, talking to informants from within the culture, and careful examination of one's own motivations and values. Clarity about oneself and one's own cultural heritage is an important dimension of preparation.

Third, respectful participation in another culture's ritual requires accommodating oneself to those practices rather than imposing one's own needs or cultural expectations upon the ritual. Good ritual guests not only learn the ways of the ritual ahead of time, they participate in them as authentically as possible. Or, if one's hosts agree, observing rather than fully participating may be appropriate to avoid intruding on sacred practices.

Fourth, an opportunity to debrief a ritual experience with those who deeply understand its meanings and broader cultural contexts has two desirable effects. Debriefing can serve to clarify and authenticate what one has just seen, noting ritual dimensions that have been overlooked and avoiding culturally biased misinterpretation of events or practices which particularly caught one's attention. Further, such debriefing can also demonstrate respect and appreciation for those persons whose ritual has enriched one's own life.

Finally, participation in, or observation of, rituals from another tradition or culture is never an end in itself. Participation in other rituals may helpfully call our attention to settings within our own lives and communities that call out for ritual attention. Such participation may suggest ways we can consider creatively ritualizing or re-ritualizing within our own cultural traditions. Lifting whole rituals from one cultural context to another may seem an easy shortcut or even appear to respect the centuries-old wisdom of another people. However, wholesale borrowing denies that rituals are connected by muscle, blood, nerve, and bone to the cultural values and history of a particular people. Observing the rituals of others more effectively helps us develop a stronger ritual sense for ourselves.

With those caveats in mind, we reflect further on the meaning of soul.

Trajectories of the Soul

In chapter 2 we described soul as a process grounded in both memory and imagination, operating at the intersection of remembered history and anticipated future. Our recorded experiences, our memories, provide content for the ways we imagine what comes next, the projected futures our brains construct. One of geometry's axioms is that two points make a line — that is, connecting two points with a straight line allows one to project that line beyond those two points in either direction. In similar ways, the brain selects points of re-membered stories and imaginatively extends those lines into the future, drawing plot lines to predict at least the immediate future. But the brain also constructs *extended* plot lines, writing stories that reach far into the future. Memories are the raw material for our imaginations.

Imagination is critical to re-membering. Each time the brain recalls a memory, it reconstructs the story from image fragments stored throughout the brain. In addition, the brain selects stories, fills in gaps, and, in extreme instances, even builds memories from scratch (see chapter 2). Those reconstructions of past events depend on the brain's current condition and needs. The brain more readily recalls events that match its owner's current mood. Present stories are associated in the brain with similar stories in the past. So the metaphor of trajectory works as well backward as it does forward; the brain can extrapolate into the past to confirm a belief it currently holds about itself. This is particularly true in depression, as we'll see below.

Neuroscientists speak of the *plasticity* of memories. Memories are recorded in strengthened synaptic connections in the brain, and the brain has remarkable capacities to modify those delicate links in the face of new experiences. This is particularly true during infancy and childhood, but the brain continues to change throughout life. Memories are no longer fixed in time. They present themselves differently, if only so slightly, each time they appear. When we attend to memories during periods of heightened expectancy, such as the ritual experiences of interest to us in this volume, those memories are particularly subject to recall and to change.

Because memories are central to who we are as persons, to our souls, we must acknowledge the *dynamic* nature of the soul. Our souls are literally transformed from moment to moment. Experience and biology are constant companions, reinforcing and shaping each other as our souls unfold. Because we reimagine our memories each time we recall them, at least the potential for change exists each time we do so. This description of personal experience calls to mind the dimensions of transition and concrescence at the heart of process theology.[3]

---

3. John Cobb Jr. and David Ray Griffin, *Process Theology: An Introductory Exposition* (Philadelphia: Westminster Press, 1976), 14–15.

Our description of memory and imagination also underscores the *uniqueness* of souls. Given that no two persons encounter identical experiences, no two persons tell or construct identical stories. Brain structures themselves are unique. In spite of the similarities of overall construction, individual brains vary, sometimes notably, from person to person.

Finally, our description of the brain's operations makes note of the *relational* nature of the brain. From the activity of individual neurons to the imaginative and nurturing capacities of the human brain, our brains seek connections. This circumstance both makes possible and requires that we live out our lives in relationship with others. We tend to think of brains, and the images and memories they produce, as private organs, encapsulated in separate skulls and bodies having little to do with other brains in other bodies. For so often we have thought of our brains as the seat of our uniqueness, but not of our belonging, when, in fact, our brains constantly engage in processes of mirroring and imagining the products of other brains (see chapter 1).

Studies of the brain's ability to imagine other minds, to re-create within itself the emotional and cognitive experiences of another, demonstrate that the brain is built for *empathy*. Under normal conditions of development, the infant brain "catches" the feelings of people around, particularly those in distress. As it matures, the brain's frontal lobes provide the capacity to regulate the internal distress such mirroring produces, consider the cognitive as well as emotional aspects of the other's experiences, and suggest appropriate responses.[4] In chapter 2, we extended this notion to counter our understandings of memory as "owned" by individuals, arguing that memories are also held in community. We are remembered as surely as we remember.

Because of memory and imagination, then, our souls are unique, dynamic, and relational processes, grounded in the structures of body and brain. In our souls, our embodied memories and imaginations are bound together, sketching and following internal maps in plotting

---

4. See, for example, Stephanie Preston and Frans B. M. de Waal, "Empathy: Its Ultimate and Proximate Bases," *Behavioral and Brain Sciences* 25 (February 2002).

our course through life. Past, present, and future interact constantly in living and in relating.

But how do our spiritual practices enable the transformations of spirit that we seek?

Ritual as Play

Our meaning-making brains are creators of their own worlds. We model in our minds the way the world is, and our minds then live in those created worlds. As we discovered in chapter 1, the brain and body respond to imagined worlds as though these worlds are real, particularly when imaginations and memories have been deeply encoded.

The worlds our brains create are social worlds just as much as they are physical worlds. We know that others around us have minds because we are aware of our own minds. Our brains come into this world with an innate, unfolding capacity not only to know that others have thoughts and feelings and intentions, but also to predict the contents of those other minds. This capacity begins very early and advances rapidly at least until age four.[5] Those images direct our behavior, both consciously and unconsciously.

Ritual practices, times, and spaces bracket our experiences so that they achieve a heightened potency, both to sustain us and to transform us. At their most effective, pastoral counseling and spiritual practices provide free spaces in which our imaginations can be both liberated and anchored. The rules of everyday living are suspended for a time. The mind is freed to play with different worlds than those it encounters in day-to-day living. Rituals frequently are enacted to accomplish something, and yet they also require that we suspend our more common need to achieve.

Worship, pastoral counseling, and spiritual direction at their best are built on the foundations of play, or what ritual scholar Ronald

---

5. Steven Pinker, *How the Mind Works* (New York: W. W. Norton, 1997), 330–31.

Grimes calls celebration.[6] By play we mean the capacity to suspend the hard and fast rules of everyday living—those tyrannical realities of life that remind us that there are consequences, now or later, for every action, thought, and feeling we experience. In ordinary time we take action to produce a result or to avoid one. In play, we participate for the sheer enjoyment of it all. We make up our world as we go, and we change it at will. We can try out new ways of being. We can try on new selves. And when one doesn't work, or when we tire of one, we can try another way of being, another self.

The meaning of play as we intend it here is different from the play of sports. Games are built on the accomplishment of some outcome, and usually on preventing someone else from accomplishing the same thing. It becomes a serious venture, though watching skilled participants — like Michael Jordan or Sammy Sosa — play a game well often convinces us that some participants actually do play! Yet sports and the kind of play that is at the heart of ritual also share defining elements. Sporting events involve construction of an artificial world with specific boundaries, like a baseball diamond, football field, or tennis court. Participants agree to rules that are different from those that apply elsewhere. If a hockey player on a city street throws a rough crosscheck on an unsuspecting pedestrian, he or she is subject to severe legal penalties! Games also mark a specific beginning and ending so all participants and observers know when the rules revert to those of the outside world.

Play and rituals, by virtue of the temporary worlds they construct, both depend on the presence of liminal space — space and time set apart. In living with a different set of rules, roles, and goals, participants live for a time in a "what if..." world. By choice, as we play or participate, we are living as though another reality were present.

---

6. Ronald L. Grimes, *Beginnings in Ritual Studies,* rev. ed. (Columbia: University of South Carolina Press, 1995), 53–56.

Living as If

Some years ago the wife of a friend, Michael, was suddenly struck by cancer and her entire stomach was removed. She underwent available medical procedures, including chemotherapy, and supplemented those with careful nutrition. The two of them also turned to the resources of their faith, participating in services for healing within their religious tradition. For some months, medical tests showed little or no further growth in sites where cancer had been previously detected. Michael and his wife knew the medical odds of full recovery were slim, and yet they remained hopeful. As months passed, she visited the office of the doctor who had done the surgery. Office staff were surprised to see her. They had never expected she would be alive six months after diagnosis of that kind of cancer, let alone a year and a half. In the midst of those days, she reported a profound experience of being healed.

As Michael described the experience to me, he acknowledged balancing within his own soul the medical realities they were facing as well as the hope for health of which they felt confident. They talked with others around the country who had survived illnesses that kill most of their victims. They participated in support and Bible study groups for others as well as for themselves. They worshiped regularly.

In the midst of a time of fear and worry, and wanting to be honest about his own concerns as well as support his and his wife's hopes, Michael spoke of "living as if" she had been healed. It was an intriguing and hopeful description of faith — a faith that acknowledged the realities of living in vulnerable bodies and, at the same time, held a vision of another reality, one of wholeness and health. It was a statement of a faith in an unseen vision to which they aspired, but one on which they dared not yet risk all of the depths of the meaning of hope. It was also a declaration of a choice — a choice to live life with a conviction of that for which they most hoped, even when hard evidence of a final cure was not available. Michael spoke of the unanticipated extension of his beloved's life as a healing in itself, regardless of how long she ultimately would survive. It was an eschatological hope.

At one level, Michael's words may sound like he was hedging his bets. His words suggest a strong wish without much empirical certainty. "Living as if" is a subjunctive phrase; those words point to a hope rather than a promise. We live as though this is true, even in the midst of our lack of clear certainty.

We all construct images of the way the world is, of what is happening around us and in us. The only reality we can actually know is the reality that our brains construct, the one we image and imagine. So Michael's decision to live "as if" is a conscious claiming of the circumstances under which we all live. We can only live in the worlds we believe are real. Though much of this believing operates below our levels of awareness, we can also make choices about the worlds we inhabit.

In ritual moments of life — those encounters when story, memory, and imagination are performed in ways that embody our own experience — we uniquely build the worlds we inhabit. When we choose to live out in our bodies and minds the realities to which we are committed, we participate in bringing about that world.

This is far from a passive experience. We do not simply sit back in padded pews and allow the Spirit to do this wonderful thing to us. Instead, we enter into the stories and movements of the Spirit as we encounter them, and we are changed by our participation. As worship leaders or as pastoral counselors, it is a central dimension of our calling to create spaces in which such movement is possible. Those whose care has been entrusted to us expect that we handle the power of ritual responsibly and faithfully, that we respect the life-giving nature of engaging ritual and avoid rituals that bore or deaden. Like our model, we come to bring life rather than death, hope rather than despair, and active participation in God's purposes.

Building Ritual Structures

So what is necessary to create such space? What makes liminal time and space different from other times and places? The first requirement is a sense of *safety*. To move into time and space for intimate engagement with the symbols of our faith and lives requires a deep trust that such imagining will be encouraged rather than punished. If worship, spiritual direction, or pastoral counseling holds too rigid a model for what we ought to experience, we are more likely to respond with either compliance or rebellion than to engage the creative capacities of our minds. Effective rituals provide structures designed to engage the symbolic, imagining self. To the degree that we require compliance in thought or outcome, we also restrict opportunities for full engagement by those most intimately involved.

There are several tensions here. Lack of structure undermines a sense of freedom as surely as too much structure does. Undirected thoughts and actions can create anxiety rather than safety. And individuals vary greatly in their need for such structure. Safety is a complicated matter but nonetheless is a necessary condition for effective ritual experience.

A second dimension of ritual space is the opposite of safety. Entering ritual space entails *risk* as well. Young boys entering rites of passage in some cultures, though not all, are subjected to some of the most terrifying experiences of their lives.[7] They confront devils, beasts, and pain along with the uncertainty of the unknown. They experience isolation that tests and refines their capacity to take care of themselves. Rites of passage are far from the idyllic experiences we sometimes imagine.

We are able to confront the risks posed by ritual experiences because of the structures of safety that are built in. In primitive cultural rites of passage, usually the elders are entrusted with the initiation processes. They are charged with responsibility for the safety of the initiates as well as for their trials. While worship, spiritual direction, and pastoral counseling are commonly less dangerous than traditional rites of passage, effective ritual leaders still provide protection as well as invitation to face that which is painful or uncomfortable.

---

7. Ronald L. Grimes, *Deeply into the Bone: Reinventing Rites of Passage* (Berkeley: University of California Press, 2000).

But how is such safety offered in the ministries of the church? How can we make worship and counseling space safe enough that worshipers and clients can confront both the grace and judgment in their lives? How can the public and private spaces where we pray and practice other spiritual disciplines be made safe enough for us to encounter the transcendent? How can we indeed "comfort the afflicted and afflict the comfortable"?

One critical way we provide safe space is to create a clear *boundary*. In our North American culture, we are generally rewarded for our hardheaded realism rather than our creative imaginations. Much of our culture is built on the values of conquest and domination. So safe time and space must be marked. It must have a beginning and ending, and those lines must be unmistakable. Unambiguous signals should alert all participants that the rules are different now. For a time we will live in a world of grace and self-reflection, a time of centering within ourselves and of connecting with each other and with God.

When the ethos of worship is indistinguishable from the ethos of coffee hour, worship has lost its power. When a pastoral counseling session is indistinguishable from a chat with a friend over coffee, opportunities for in-depth encounter have probably been missed. (Of course the relatively easy conversation in early counseling sessions may be an appropriate way to lower undue anxiety and begin to build a trusting relationship in which deeper conversations may occur. Likewise, more casual forms of worship provide less threatening avenues into the experience of encounter with God for persons coming to church for the first time, individuals returning to church after a long absence, and those unable to connect with more formal or liturgical structures.) A seminary colleague of mine jokes that coffee hour may well be the "third sacrament." Certainly none of us would want to forego the importance of casual fellowship either before or after profound experiences of worship. But the power of ritual is in its set-apartness. When transitions into worship or counseling become so fluid that they become indistinguishable from the ordinary time out of which they emerge, we lose ritual's most effective properties.

Closing Moments

Boundary refers not only to beginnings but also to endings. The distinctiveness of ritual experiences depends on an awareness that this ritual too will come to an end. Rituals both mimic the reality of life itself and transcend life's limits. We are able to confront our deepest selves and an otherwise frightening reality of grace when we know that we cannot, or must not, remain there forever. We are more likely to enter a dark tunnel when we know there is light at the other end. Ritual experiences do not last forever, just as Jesus and the three disciples' experience on the Mount of Transfiguration came to an end. There is inevitably a return to the valley and the demands of the world (Matt. 17:1–18). The world that was left behind awaits our return, and the rules of living in that world have not substantially changed while we have been residing elsewhere.

Effective counselors and worship leaders understand that the ending of ritual time requires preparation. If the early and middle portions of ritual experience are designed to welcome us into new worlds and new places, then the closing minutes of ritual experiences demand that we prepare for return to the world the way it is. That happens neither automatically nor quickly. The closing moments of ritual experience are not times for new in-depth encounters with the sacred or with the self. They are times for disconnection and reconnection, for transition back to the places from which people have come.

Counselors, however, frequently encounter clients who bring up significant material as the end of the session approaches. This behavior usually stems from one of two causes: often it is a desire to get frightening matters on the table without having to confront in-depth the implications or shame-inducing dimensions of those issues. Clients suspect it will be easier to approach these vital issues in the next session once both counselor and counselee have had a chance to consider the matter. At other times, the client wishes (consciously or unconsciously) to extend rather than end the session. In either case, the experienced counselor maintains the structure of the session by ending on time so the carefully developed structures of the counseling relationship remain in place for the future.

Similarly, worship participants who have immersed themselves in profound experiences of the sacred may be reluctant to leave holy time and space behind. They feel unprepared for return to the world. Disconnecting from the intimacy and awe of worship is necessary before re-engaging the world. Closing moments of worship and counseling alike require two particular types of preparation. Integration of the experiences participants have encountered is key. This may involve a brief summary and review of what one has experienced, either by spoken word or in silent reflection. Integration may invite persons to imagine scenarios in which the insights of the ritual are played out. It may employ gestures or movements that embody new ways of being, such as kneeling in prayerful reverence, standing in anticipation of God's work in the world, or grasping the hands of those around in solidarity with community.

But endings also require a turning around, a facing into the world one has temporarily left behind. We leave behind the sanctuary or consultation room and, in at least some small way, grieve its loss. We may leave with anticipation, relief, or dread, but we clearly mark that the boundaried time of ritual experience is now over. Such parting not only smooths the transition from ritual to nonritual space. It also prepares us for ritual experiences in the future.

Unfinished Business

Rituals are marked by their beginnings and their endings. Yet the work of most rituals never ends. Rituals that open us to the creative potential of any given moment can't simply be "put back in the box." Whether we speak of worship, pastoral care, or covenant groups, ritual actions immerse us in the creative significance of one moment and so unlock for us the potential of all moments. Once we have consciously imagined our memories and remembered our futures, our history and that which is yet to come are irrevocably joined together. Once we have heard or told new stories, in the very act of creating new experiences, we are now alert to the reality that each encounter we have with the world from now on is as meaning-full as the one we have just experienced.

Because our souls emerge from the dynamic interplay between memory and imagination, deep ritual experiences strengthen them. Like muscles that have been exercised, our souls grow stronger and more prepared for their next encounter. Souls that have engaged a new reality are on the lookout for new possibilities in other places, in other stories. Indeed, souls that have encountered liberation of the imagination long to find it in other places. Ritual experiences are both self-contained (they have a definite beginning and ending) and open — their effects spill over into life beyond those specific encounters.

Having noted the critical presence of play (living as if), boundaries, and unfinished business in all ritual, we turn now to the practice of pastoral counseling, exploring in more detail the roles that memory, imagination, and story have to play.

Pastoral Counseling and Ritual

We pastoral counselors are not inclined to think of our work as ritual. We have tended for several reasons to separate our work and self-understanding from the public life and ritual activities of congregations and other institutions. Rituals are frequently public events and depend on shared meanings and values of the congregation, denomination, or religious tradition rather than private conversations that give expression to the meanings of an individual or a family. Rituals are instruments of belonging, proclaiming our solidarity with others more than our difference and uniqueness. Finally, with their emphasis on making conscious the unconscious and cognitive understanding, psychoanalytically oriented psychotherapies in particular have avoided ritual as a process that undermines healing through "acting out" unconscious processes rather than verbalizing them. Such performance arguably makes feelings unavailable to rational understanding. The assumption has been that talking about experiences — that is, categorizing them through the conventions of language — is critical to understanding and healing. In neuropsychological terms, underlying feelings have not been adequately processed by neocortical structures but rather have passed primarily through subcortical processes. Hence, no insight. In addition to those theoretical matters, legitimate concerns about the abuse of touch in the counseling relationship have further distanced counselors from the body.

Yet the very structures of pastoral counseling depend on ritual processes. The liminal nature of a pastoral counseling session acknowledges that it is a transitional space in which different rules and expectations apply. It is clearly marked by a beginning and ending so that both counselor and client learn what to expect from each other. The liminal space of counseling sessions is designed to promote change and growth in personal identity.

A critical difference, of course, is the nonscripted nature of the performance of pastoral counseling. *What* each person says is not dictated. But how they say it clearly has expected parameters. More controversial is the performance or planning of rituals during a counseling session. Pastoral counselors vary a great deal in their willingness to employ ritual as part of the counseling process. Therapists trained in psychoanalytic traditions are less likely to make use of ritual, while those trained primarily in family systems or cognitive-behavioral approaches are likely to find rituals more appealing. Theoretical orientation and personal comfort are critical to decisions about the direct employment of any technique, but particularly in matters of ritual performance.[8]

---

8. David A. Hogue, "Shelters and Pathways: Ritual and Pastoral Counseling," in *Journal of Supervision and Training in Ministry* 19 (1999): 57–67.

Rewriting History

In chapter 2 we discussed memory's vulnerabilities — its limits and apparent "failures." Here we look more carefully at the gift of memory's fragility, the possibilities for healing and transformation that are a direct consequence of memory's plasticity. When we stop thinking of memories as fixed records of an immutable past and begin to see them as interpretive schemas that are inevitably partial and shaped by the needs of the moment, we open new possibilities for change.

How often do clients enter a counseling relationship despairing of the fact that "I can never change what happened. I can never undo what I did or what was done to me." Possibilities for change lie in reconsidering the notion of historical "facts" that are distinct from the meanings we have made of them and from the interpretations with which we encoded them.

To be sure, we cannot have much confidence in "made-to-order memories." We cannot with integrity or conviction simply decide what we want the details of an earlier event to be and then proceed to rebuild the story. Despite memory's plasticity, its general shape must be dependable for us to trust it and for us to rely on any sense of the reality and continuity it represents. But a healthy sense of skepticism, a hermeneutic of suspicion, paves the way to deeper understandings of another's story — and of our own stories.

In counseling, it is not the helper's task, especially initially, to communicate a sense of distrust or disbelief. Structuring a counseling relationship requires sensitive support and measured curiosity, not disbelief. But as a counseling relationship develops, questions like, "I wonder what else was taking place then?" or "How could this have happened and not that?" can introduce clients to a healthy curiosity about the functioning of their own memories. None of these questions can be asked before a solid sense of trust between counselor and client has been developed.

Once such a question has been raised and received, several options are open. Sometimes the story is missing details that can be recovered or considered that shift the emotional meaning of an otherwise painful event. Details that make no sense in the overall scheme of the story can be explored.

Narrative pastoral theologians speak of counternarrative when they refer to the small events or motifs in a story that do not fit the primary themes — those stories of subtle resistance by a victim of oppression or abuse, those moves of assertion by a self-perceived passive participant in life, those acts of care for another by someone who sees himself as isolated and selfish. Looking for exceptions often enables client and counselor to undermine restrictive themes and begin constructing more liberating stories.

Remembering Feelings

Remembered stories are more than the recalled images and reconstructed narratives clients bring to the consultation room or that they recite to themselves throughout the course of a day. As we noted in chapter 2, memories are encoded and recalled with emotional tone that is stored in the emotional memory systems of the brain. Though they are recorded and recalled by separate brain structures, these emotional dimensions of memory are tightly associated with particular stories with two important results. First, when we recall an event, we generally also reexperience its emotional impact. Stories and their associated feelings appear to be inseparably bound together, though emotional memories may be experienced in the absence of their autobiographical memories. In addition, emotional memories may persist long after we have forgotten the narratives that prompted them.[9] Some unexplainable feelings may in fact be the result of stories that persist in unconscious memory or of unconscious goals that have not been met. A second consequence is that, when we experience a particular feeling, an encoded story may well be dragged into consciousness along with the feeling.

---

9. Joseph LeDoux, *The Emotional Brain: The Mysterious Underpinnings of Emotional Life* (New York: Touchstone, 1996), 203.

Pastoral counseling, consistent with its psychodynamic roots, has understood healing to result from the recall of emotionally significant experiences within the context of a safe interpersonal relationship. The discharge of feeling during recollections is not in itself considered therapeutic. "Working through" more specifically involves making unconscious memories conscious and thereby weakening their power over current emotional life.

Cognitive theorists have argued that thoughts influence feelings. By altering the self-talk of suffering persons, problematic feelings and behaviors may be altered. Neuroscientist Joseph LeDoux's description of the brain's fear system suggests that emotional memories never fully disappear. Nevertheless, autobiographic memories stored in the neocortex of the brain may be altered in ways that minimize the emotional impact of traumatic memories. LeDoux sees cognitive therapies as the most helpful in dealing with anxiety and depression, though he notes that psychoanalytic therapies also show evidence of modifying amygdala-based, fearful input to the cortex.

Discussion of the brain and remembered feelings often prompts discussion of recent psychotherapeutic techniques believed to change brain functioning directly. An intriguing, if controversial, approach that has been found to be effective with victims of post-traumatic stress disorder is Eye Movement Desensitization and Reprocessing (EMDR).[10] Critics caricature EMDR for its use of rapid hand movements designed to direct clients' eye movements back and forth during recall of emotional memories, and yet it is one of the most extensively researched treatments for PTSD. The method relies on recall of emotionally significant body sensations more than on specific narrative descriptions, yet images and stories remain integral to the approach. While the exact neurology of EMDR is still undergoing exploration, proponents of EMDR suggest that "bilateral

---

10. Francine Shapiro and Margot Silk Forrest, *Eye Movement Desensitization and Reprocessing: The Breakthrough Therapy for Overcoming Anxiety, Stress, and Trauma* (New York: Basic Books, 1997).

stimulation" of the brain during recall of traumatic memories weakens emotional memories so that narratives can be recalled without anxiety-producing consequences. Anecdotal reports by therapists and clients alike suggest that EMDR deserves continued serious evaluation and consideration.

Depression, Anxiety, and Story Trajectories

Depression and anxiety have multiple determinants. No single cause can shoulder all the blame for these common human experiences. Anxiety and depression range from mildly uncomfortable to severely disabling or even life threatening. Threats to life can be either direct through suicide or indirect through contributions to damaging behaviors, cardiovascular and gastric diseases, and other physiological consequences.

Life narratives, and particularly our understanding of story trajectories, also provide a way to consider these particular disorders of mood. Depression, for instance, is characterized by a sense of dread and foreboding, a sensed loss of alternatives or choices for living and loss of hope. Such a projected outlook can be understood in part as the brain's projections into the future from stories recalled from the past. A man recently divorced for the third time might understandably imagine a future alone or a series of painful rejections. A competent woman passed over twice for promotions will likely confront images of glass ceilings and a future of professional frustrations. Recalled stories of abuse or unmet needs during childhood and adolescence are particularly likely to produce future stories of limited or painful alternatives.

Such trajectories occur in at least two ways. Recalling limiting or painful memories may prompt the brain to imagine future stories of hopelessness. In this case, future stories themselves lead to feelings of foreboding and dread. But because the brain also selects and interprets events from memory, persons already depressed based on current circumstances or biochemical changes in the brain are more likely to recall life events in which they felt as they do now. Depressed brains find stories that confirm their depression.[11] Pastoral counselors commonly hear depressed persons recall with an obsessive persistence events of loss or failure in the past.

It is possible then to think of depression as the dominance of memory over imagination. Remembered events of loss or failure block the imagination from considering alternatives, and, because the imagination is the seat of hope (see chapter 1), the tyranny of particular memories over life's trajectories damages or destroys the soul. In another sense, however, depression also coopts the imagination, directing it to select particular memories that confirm feelings of hopelessness or to color or construct them if necessary. The imagination has lost its freedom to play.

In anxiety, the opposite is true. In certain forms of anxiety the imagination has created future scenarios that may also have their roots in the memories of particular events. But in the case of anxiety, the brain constructs images of fear and terror and responds with the limbic system's primitive fight-or-flight response. Similar to the patterns observed in depression, states of anxiety induced either by storied memories or biochemical disruptions may prompt the meaning-making brain to imagine particular catastrophic scenarios to explain its state of agitation. Anxious persons often report an inability to recall events of peace or success. When they do, they often cannot hold those memories to calm or reassure themselves. In this case, the imagination has run away, loosed from the cross-check of memories. The brain is constructing too many alternatives or scenarios unsupported by reason or memory.

Grief

Loss is a universal human experience that also helps us further comprehend the interlocked work of memory and imagination. Our experiences of loss are grounded in the initial separation from mother

---

11. Daniel L. Schacter, *Searching for Memory: The Brain, the Mind, and the Past* (New York: Basic Books, 1996), 211.

we experienced at birth and represent a cry that we share with other mammals. Those experiences of separation served as the grounds for our first acts of meaning making and the roots of consciousness.[12] In grief, we remember and imagine so we can make sense of what has happened and what is to come. While we usually associate the word "grief" with the death of a loved one, grief applies as well to other significant losses.[13] Remembering is our primary activity in the early stages of grief following the loss of a loved one. Recent memories dominate our recollections at first, recalling our latest interactions, such as an illness, accident, or events leading up to death. Over time, we gather a broader range of memories, retelling the story of our relationship with the one who is lost. Imagination participates in the selection and reconstruction of those stories.

Imagination increasingly takes its place in the experiencing of loss as the griever begins to construct images of life in the absence of the loved one. Such scenarios are at first too painful for most persons to hold for long; earlier story trajectories have not yet been relinquished, and new trajectories have not been formed. While extended illness or age may prompt individuals to begin writing new future stories well in advance of a death, the finality of death still must be remembered and incorporated before new trajectories can be firmly grasped.

The process of storytelling in grief is to be encouraged. Impatience with grief in the form of encouragement to "get on with life" can disrupt the central activity of memory in grief. Such memories may well function initially as an attempt to hold on to one who is gone. Yet such remembering is the substance of our attempts to consolidate our stories and experiences of life with another, to incorporate those stories into our own souls. Stories function in the transitional space between what was and what will be, much as a child seeks comfort in the presence of transitional objects during separation from the

---

12. James Ashbrook, "The Cry for the Other: The Biocultural Womb of Human Development," *Zygon* 29, no. 3 (September 1994): 297–314.

13. Kenneth R. Mitchell and Herbert Anderson, *All Our Losses, All Our Griefs: Resources for Pastoral Care* (Philadelphia: Westminster Press, 1983), 35–52.

life-giving support of caregivers.[14] As such stories are more deeply
encoded by virtue of their retelling, the brain is gradually freed to
construct future stories that include the other's absence.

The Price of Forgetting

Memories of painful or disturbing stories that distort our images of
self are only part of the problem. Gaps in our personal stories lead
to a sense of incompleteness or of uncertainty about why we do the
things we do and feel the things we feel. Repression and suppression,
those mechanisms by which we forget memories that continue to hurt
us, cloud the pictures we have of our own lives. Unconscious stories
constitute parts of the self we have not claimed.

Our forgetting does not always seem to be a choice, or at least
a conscious one. Some forgetting is automatic, even unwanted, but
nevertheless real. Recovering those memories, and eventually reclaiming the power we have allowed those memories to have over our lives,
leads to healing. Unconscious, painful memories are the stuff of spiritual and emotional sickness. It is a given that the wounding chapters
of our stories, those that are not integrated into our sense of who we
are, are damaging to our souls. Still other memories are lost through
the ravages of disease, but here we are concerned with memories that
are lost by otherwise healthy brains.

Such forgetting appears self-protective. We "choose" to forget stories that don't fit who we imagine ourselves to be, or stories that
hurt all over again as we imagine ourselves in that state of helpless
victimization (or willful perpetration). But such forgetting may also
protect others for whom protection is not deserved. Forgetting too
often protects perpetrators rather than those who may be damaged
by those persons now or in the future.

Counselors know well the time and trust required before wounded
individuals can risk confronting untold stories in their lives. Just as

---

14. Ashbrook, "The Cry for the Other," 300.

we encode events in memory to meet our needs at that moment, we also recall or reconstruct them in ways that meet our current needs of the new moment. Those needs may or may not correspond to the "facts" of the events in the first place, at least as we usually think of facts.

Critical listening is called for. We listen respectfully and carefully to another's story, noting the gaps and "where the feelings are." We walk another fine line between empathic entry into that story and maintaining a vital sense of ourselves as a separate feeling and thinking human being. Truly joining others in their suffering requires that we maintain a sense of ourselves at the same time we are looking at life through the eyes of another — always a delicate balance.

Listening to the stories of persons in pain is more than hard work — it is dangerous work. Stories told for the first time may undermine the cover stories that have been developed to deny them and isolate them from conscious awareness. Listening in these circumstances requires that the counselor be truly able to receive disturbing and painful stories, entering into the pain of another without being destroyed by it.

Yet invitation and openness are only part of what is required. We balance a sense of invitation with a careful avoidance of coercion or permission that may lead a client later to withdraw in shame. Clients readily feel the expectations of counselors to reveal their most shameful secrets. Respectful counselors know that clients need to learn to judge their own readiness for such disclosure. Communicating regularly that we are ready to hear when the client is ready to speak helps achieve this balance.

We listen to believe. But at the same time we hold a critical ear, understanding the ways memory is constructed and the pitfalls of literalism. We watch particularly for stories in which other persons are either idols or villains and consider whether this client is likely to take actions outside the counseling relationship that could provoke denial or even retribution. It is once again a delicate balance — measuring respectful belief with critical reflection, acknowledging the current status of a memory with the possibilities of memory transformation in the future.

Three dimensions of listening are particularly crucial in pastoral counseling. The first is an *educative* process, experiencing with clients over time the vulnerabilities of remembered stories and the possibilities for their reconsideration. Again the key is respectful consideration, moving gradually toward critical reflection. Demonstrating trust in the client's integrity is vital, and only once that trust has been established do we open the questions that lead to deeper understanding. "I believe the gist of your story and will continue to listen for its meaning." To embody this relational tension, counselors must have experienced the consideration and reconstruction of their own memories as well as the internal sense of personal confidence that comes through careful reflection.

The second dimension of this process is a *deeper sense of certainty* that develops as the story is told. The risks are clear — we can believe stories that are not verifiable. But another consequence is that, as we retell stories that have previously been unvoiced and yet describe real events, clients deepen their conviction of the truth. Rehearsal can become a vital preparation and vehicle for truth telling. One of the messages that abused persons have often received — sadly both from perpetrators and from families and friends in whom they may have tried to confide, not to mention stories told in the media or trials portrayed on TV — is that no one will believe them. Even when their sense of conviction about their memories is strong, they live with the justifiable fear that they will not be believed and that they will be humiliated and isolated even further for the telling of those stories.

Even as I write these chapters, the stories of untold numbers of young men who have suffered sexual abuse at the hands of trusted priests are bombarding the media. (And Protestant churches dare not point fingers, because our handling of clergy sexual misconduct has been equally reprehensible.) In too many of those stories, where the church negotiated a settlement, one of the central stipulations was that victims would not tell the stories outside the tribunals where their stories were voiced. The result? The victims are revictimized. Consequently, chances to retell and work through those stories were also taken from them. In recent months, many victims have broken that silence.

Memories Shared

A third dimension of memory to which we alluded in chapter 2 involves the communal nature of memory. Memories are not the sole possession of single brains. We hold memories of and for each other as well. The increasingly familiar stories of memory loss experienced by people with Alzheimer's disease have prompted many of us to reconsider our individualistic notions of memory. The irony of a dying mind in a living body has struck many as uniquely tragic and revealing of our dependency on our own memories.

At the seminary where I teach, we offer a course in ritual in teaching and care. We regularly ask students to develop a ritual for families losing a parent to Alzheimer's. Inevitably they struggle with how to embody family and personal memories in ways that acknowledge the reality of loss, along with the continuing meaning of this person to the family. The rituals commonly have at least two dimensions: There is a telling (and often recording on video or audiotape) of stories, as much for the family as for the patient, and there is the creation or display of images which represent this person's life — pictures, meaningful objects, and mementos. One "family" hung pictures of family members on a mobile that could then be taken to the parents' new setting as a physical replacement for lost memories. Such rituals are often helpful for the family — they may well be helpful for the Alzheimer's patient. But they do dramatize the importance of memories and, when performed before memory loss is too advanced, can assure patients that the memories they can no longer maintain for themselves will be held by those who love them.

Chaplains Jim and Susan Gullickson tell the story of Jim's mother's Alzheimer's illness in the mid-1980s. Because all of the children lived at some distance, they considered several options for her care. The family finally chose a nursing home in Freeman, South Dakota, the town where Jim's parents had retired after selling their nearby farm. Not only did they remain close to the land on which they had lived and worked, the nursing staff had also been born and raised in that area. As Stena Gullickson's memory began to fail, staff members were able to help fill in the blanks and even as her memory deteriorated further, were motivated to "treat her like the person she was."[15]

Such a reinterpretation of the meaning of memory depends ultimately on the presence of communities. Where we are responsible for memories on our own — their vitality and their continuation — those memories are inevitably doomed to disappear. And yet when we are the objects as well as the subjects of remembering, those memories are deepened and continued because they are shared. In so doing, we anchor our sense of being remembered as well.

Pastoral counseling provides a temporary community in which persons voice the stories of their lives. Some of those stories may never have been told before, while others may have been repeated so often that even the storyteller is tired of them. This is one reason the ending of a counseling relationship can be difficult, particularly when that relationship has provided a deeply moving encounter over time. Clients may feel they are leaving behind the treasure of memories they have spoken, recovered, and constructed and fear those memories will no longer be available. One of the vital tasks of ending a counseling relationship is the review of the story of the therapy itself, reminding both counselor and client of the shared stories that will continue to be remembered.

Counseling relationships are temporary, small communities. But larger webs of relationship, such as communities of faith, also serve as memory holders and as providers of transforming images. In chapter 6 we turn to worship and spiritual disciplines as practices of remembering and imagining.

---

15. Susan Gullickson, personal communication, August 19, 2002.

Chapter 6

AND THEN...
The Brain and Spiritual Disciplines

The performance of narrative and gesture... creates the life-giving memory of God in the community of the faithful, who carry out the grace of that covenant in the world.

—Bruce T. Morrill[1]

Public stories and rituals define our communities of faith. Personal stories and rituals define us as unique selves. When we worship well, our stories and God's story converge. We see and hear our own narratives played out in the stories of faith, and we glimpse our personal stories from the vantage of God's larger story. Yet too often we do not recognize ourselves in the acts and stories of worship.[2] Worship becomes an exercise in obligation rather than participation, a chance to see friends rather than to encounter God. Resolving such a dilemma is far beyond the scope of this volume. Yet our understanding of imagination, memory, and ritual suggests several implications for more meaningful worship.

The role of memory and imagination would seem to be radically different from what we have been considering in pastoral counseling. Worship leaders, unlike pastoral counselors, seldom have access to the stories and images that participants are engaging as they worship, except as they learn about them later. Sheer numbers (in most cases),

---

1. Bruce T. Morrill, *Anamnesis as Dangerous Memory: Political and Liturgical Theology in Dialogue* (Collegeville, Minn.: Liturgical Press, 2000), 186.
2. Herbert Anderson and Edward Foley, *Mighty Stories, Dangerous Rituals: Weaving Together the Human and the Divine* (Los Angeles: Jossey-Bass, 1998), 42.

let alone the structures of worship itself, make such access impossible. Worship is at once a corporate and private matter.

Yet worship is also an intentionally structured experience of remembering and narrative. But rather than beginning with the re-membered stories and images of individual persons, the starting point for worship is the stories of the community, understood at the same time to be the stories of God. Reading of Scriptures or other sacred texts, recitation of creeds, preaching, and above all sacraments such as baptism and communion all are acts of remembrance — "Do this in remembrance of me."

As our family watched a movie together several years ago, my wife and I (two English majors) began criticizing its plot line and disap-pointing character development. Disturbed by this disruption of his viewing enjoyment, my son could take it no longer. "It's a movie. Don't analyze it!" he finally blurted out. Ever since, that phrase has served as a friendly reminder when any of us falls into the trap of analysis when synthesis is called for. When stories are well told, we are invited into them. Our empathizing brains imitate and identify with characters as plots unfold. Images conscious and unconscious are formed and re-formed as we live for a time in the world of story. Such an experience relies on the imaginative and empathic skills of the brain far more than on our capacities for critical analysis. Ab-stractions and analysis during worship lean too heavily to the left — the brain's left hemisphere, that is. Our brains are natural storytellers. The left hemisphere's interpreter engages the right brain's comprehen-sion of context and meaning. As we noted in chapter 1, our brains automatically mirror the movements we create in our imaginations — we embody the stories we hear.

Story-rich worship and preaching engage brain and body in ways abstract concepts cannot. Because the brain thinks in stories, it rec-ognizes stories and focuses attention. Because our brains routinely fill in details, we need only supply enough detail to make the story vital and credible. In a culture that has become passive in its entertain-ment, habituated to a Sesame Street, thirty-second sequence of simple thoughts and plots, our brains (and spirits) can become starved for the exercise of story listening. We can become lazy in our capacities to enter into the lives of others, except perhaps for those in soap operas (daytime or primetime) and reality TV. Worship that allows us to enter the story of another serves as exercise for the imagination.

Ritual Honesty

Because of ritual's power to transform, those who facilitate ritual are accountable for the ways they wield its power. Participation in ritual can be coerced or manipulated. Expecting public participation in pledges to a national flag or emotionally coercing public faith commitments make authentic responses impossible, producing more damage than wholeness. Worship settings above all should be places of hospitality rather than demand. Pastoral theologian Elaine Ramshaw has described ways public worship can violate the ethic of ritual honesty.[3] Because worship depends so heavily on symbol rather than on the precision that results from careful language, individuals bring their own memories and meanings to any worship experience and to any particular symbolic object or gesture. It is neither desirable nor possible to achieve anything else. While rituals draw us together in community, conformity is not the agenda of worship. Transforming encounter with God and community is the hoped-for result.

At the same time, worship is not always a comfortable experience, any more than is the pastoral counseling office. The stories we hear, remember, and enact, both public and private, are often enough disturbing rather than reassuring. Pastoral theologian Herbert Anderson and liturgical theologian Ed Foley make use of New Testament scholar John Dominic Crossan's paradoxical notions of myth and parable to describe the distinct ways persons and communities shape their stories. Myth refers to stories in which conflicting opposites are reconciled. Everything comes out all right. Parables, on the other

---

3. Elaine Ramshaw, *Ritual and Pastoral Care* (Minneapolis: Fortress Press, 1987), 26–28.

hand, move the opposite direction, introducing contradiction where once reconciliation or harmony was assumed.[4]

Worship that recounts only stories with happy endings also commits ritual dishonesty. Participants fail to find reflections of their own stories in the stories of the tradition, concluding finally that they do not belong or that religion consists of fairy tales presented as "true" stories for gullible and/or needy people. Sermon illustrations that normalize only intact, heterosexual nuclear families ultimately condemn those who are single, divorced, or gay. Inspirational stories of miraculous physical healing due to persistent prayer may well introduce doubt or guilt in the man whose wife recently died of cancer. Heroic stories of persistent faith in the face of catastrophe may do the same for those who struggle with honest doubts about faith. On the other hand, stories that honestly name the brokenness, disruption, and suffering of human beings go far to include those who are otherwise marginalized. Indeed, they include us all.

Worship and the Body

In chapters 1 and 2 we noted that when the brain observes any object in the environment, it invariably records the body's relationship to that object at the same time. How close is it? Is it moving toward me or away from me? Is it threatening or attractive? These are the automatic, immediate concerns of the brain. We also noted that the brain is constantly monitoring the intricate positions and movements of limbs and muscles, interpreting and adjusting their activity. When the body performs certain actions or gestures, the brain automatically translates the meaning of that activity into a feeling.[5]

Our brains take care of this business well below the level of conscious awareness. In fact, in some cases, only after we have performed

---

4. Anderson and Foley, *Mighty Stories, Dangerous Rituals*, 12–16.
5. Antonio Damasio, *The Feeling of What Happens: Body and Emotion in the Making of Consciousness* (New York: Harcourt Brace, 1999); Joseph LeDoux, *The Emotional Brain: The Mysterious Underpinnings of Emotional Life* (New York: Touchstone, 1996), 302.

certain acts do we actually become aware of our intent to do so.[6] Neuroscientists refer to this as a bottom-up process. But the process works in the other direction as well. Our conscious images also influence our bodies as we described in chapter 1. This is a top-down process.

So why do we pay so little attention to what worshipers will be experiencing in their bodies? Given that the brain records and takes its own cues from the body's movements, why do we not more carefully think through the forms of gesture, posture, and movement that can most likely help worshipers experience awe, reverence, and peace? One of the reasons we frequently avoid movement is that we differ in the emotional responses we have to physical activity. Some persons experience vulnerability during dance or other movement, while others find liberating expression. At the same time, because all humans are embodied, our movements carry many shared meanings.

We sense, remember, and imagine through our bodies. Therefore posture, emotional state, and movement are central to our experiences of ritual. Yet in most mainline Protestant congregations, movement is severely restricted. Even inviting people to move with music they are singing brings embarrassed stares and feet firmly planted in place. Highly liturgical traditions and many African American churches make substantial use of gesture, movement, and verbal participation by all members of the congregation. Memories are most easily recalled when the emotional and physical conditions are similar to those in which those memories first occurred. So effective worship enables participants to move and gesture in ways that will evoke those memories so they can be revisited and more deeply available for transformation in worship.

Our review of ritual in chapter 4 noted that the tempos and rhythms of worship more or less effectively serve the purposes of uniting us with each other and with God. We cannot speak of body without acknowledging the central role of music and the subliminal

---

6. Michael Gazzaniga, *The Mind's Past* (Berkeley: University of California Press, 1998), 73.

rhythms of speech in worship. When we recall that worship like other ritual activity is performance, we more carefully attend to the impact our timing and movement has on worshipers. We carefully consider how those movements are appropriate to the attitudes into which we are inviting people.

Finally, the role of the senses in forming the images that shape our internal mental worlds deserves one last note. Sensory-rich worship that employs not only sight and sound, but touch and taste and smell as well, provides a more fully embodied sense of the presence of God. Despite Protestants' historic aversion to the "smells and bells" of liturgical practice, in fact our sense of smell is most effective at triggering memories and provoking symbolic expressions!

Transformative worship celebrates the bodies in which we "live and move and have our being," not for themselves, but as instruments of worship and as temples of God. Our brains are the theaters where we sense, remember, and imagine ourselves as the body of Christ. Effective worship literally incorporates us into that Body. Fortunately, worship does not shoulder the work of transformation alone. The creative work of the Spirit finds other expressions as well.

Spiritual Practices and the Brain

Public worship and pastoral counseling (as a subdiscipline of pastoral care) are distinct practices of the church that nevertheless share the common goal of nurturing persons in their love of God and neighbor. In that sense, both are subsets of the broader category of spiritual practices, which also includes such activities as meditation, spiritual direction, and devotional Bible study. Because each of these activities is directed toward assisting persons on the path to growth in relationship to self, others, and God, the roles of memory, imagination, and ritual are equally essential. Each deserves extensive attention. Here we briefly suggest implications of ritual, memory, and imagination for implementing these practices.

Spiritual Direction

Spiritual direction enjoys a long history, stretching from the earliest days of the church to the current era.[7] Roman Catholic, Orthodox, and Anglican traditions have been most hospitable to, and competent in, spiritual direction, though in recent years members of other Christian traditions have developed both interest and competence in the practice. A rapprochement between pastoral counseling and spiritual direction has been under way for several years.[8] Like pastoral counseling, spiritual direction normally takes place in a one-to-one setting or in small groups. Conversation focuses on the directee's experiences and growth, and critical listening is vital. Spiritual direction distinguishes itself from pastoral counseling (1) in its focus on spiritual growth rather than the psychological health of persons, (2) by its reliance on biblical and mystic models rather than on the psychotherapeutic metaphors that undergird most pastoral counseling, and (3) in its efforts to minimize transference through its focus on the client's relationship with God (see the chart on p. 188). At the same time, many spiritual directors are gaining expertise in psychological disciplines, just as an increasing number of pastoral counselors have become students of spiritual direction.

In regard to human experiences of memory and imagination, spiritual direction has several advantages over other forms of care. Spiritual direction shares with pastoral counseling the ritual structure of sessions — the provision of liminal space within which judgment is suspended and the imagination is free of the demands of productivity or immediate consequence. Personal stories are told. Unlike pastoral counseling, where explicit theological frames of reference may or may not be employed, spiritual direction explicitly interweaves personal stories with stories of the faith tradition. Questions like "Where do you see God at work in those events?" or "What is God calling

---

7. Martin Thornton, "History and Traditions of Spiritual Direction," in Rodney J. Hunter, ed., *Dictionary of Pastoral Care and Counseling* (Nashville: Abingdon Press, 1990), 1210–13.

8. Alan Jones, "Spiritual Direction and Pastoral Care," in Hunter, *Dictionary of Pastoral Care and Counseling,* 1213–15.

Psychotherapy, Counseling, and Spiritual Direction

	Psychotherapy	*Counseling*	*Spiritual Direction*
Focus	Self	Problem	Self-Before-God (or God)
Goal	Self-awareness; Integration; Working through of transference (early life experiences)	Decision making; Skills development; Behavior change	Deepened relationship with God
Arena	Unconscious	Conscious	Spiritual/Moral
Result	Character structure change	Problem resolution	Communion; Fruits of the Spirit
Frequency	1–5x week	2–4x month	Variable (1 x month)
Length	2–5+ years	1–12 sessions	Variable (lifelong)
Importance of Theory	Very	Somewhat	Focus on praxis; Bible Theological Traditions
Approaches	Psychodynamic; Family Systems; Cognitive-behavioral	Same — but emphasis on Conscious aspects of experience	Several Text is person, life experiences
Caregiver Training	Supervised clinical training (3–6 years)	Supervised clinical training (2+ years)	Supervised academic and clinical training in spiritual direction 1–3 years
Caregiver Credentials	State licensure (psychology, social work, counseling); National certification	State licensure National certification	Certification (Institutes)

you to do?" are central and explicitly place individual stories within the broader context of God's activity. Spiritual direction shares the primacy of the divine story that characterizes worship with opportunities for engaging the individual stories characteristic of pastoral counseling.

Spiritual direction is also historically more committed to participation in ritual, both within sessions and in activities recommended to directees. Such a framework vitally engages both memory and imagination in processes of "soul tending." Personal stories are reconstructed in their telling and hearing, and new contexts for past, present, and future become possible. In a process that closely parallels the deconstruction or counternarrative of narrative therapy, new characters (such as God) are welcomed into past and future stories and new plots envisioned, opening opportunities for new relationships with self and other. As past stories are rewritten, new trajectories for future stories become possible.

Spiritual direction works intentionally with faith stories from the directee's own religious tradition. Thus the presence and activity of God may be detected in stories that previously have been seen as divorced from God. As in worship, we might speculate further that associations are being made between the neuronal networks that store a personal narrative and those that store a faith narrative. Therefore, when either the personal or faith story is recalled, the other is recalled with it, thus transforming both the personal story and the communal story of faith.

Spiritual direction's centuries-long history and accumulated wisdom provide it with a unique place among the church's practices of care. Spiritual direction is particularly effective when the imagination is challenged and exercised as a directee struggles to discern the activity and presence of God in ways the senses cannot directly comprehend. Congruent with its focus on discernment rather than diagnosis and treatment, spiritual direction is most effective when it invites the imagination to look for the unexpected in both past and future stories. In addition, effective spiritual direction attends to ritual practices and so strengthens a sense of the ritual rhythms of life and transition. Helping directees approach rituals with a sense of expectancy and immerse themselves in the sensory richness of liturgy is a unique opportunity for spiritual direction. Though spiritual direction has been criticized at times for its individualism, attention to liturgical and other ritual practices encourages and embodies participation in the larger community.

Small Groups

Other spiritual practices may take place without the presence of an "expert," though participants may helpfully be trained in their use. Small groups that gather regularly for Bible study or mutual encouragement and who hold each other accountable for participation through covenants or other agreements constitute a spiritual practice that has survived the test of time. Small group meetings provide opportunities for individuals to share personal concerns and weave together personal stories with the divine story, enterprises that are enhanced by shared commitments to faith and group members' diverse perspectives. Small groups also are free to adapt or develop ritual practices that affirm both the group's uniqueness and its connection to the larger religious tradition.

Attending to the ritual practices used in group meetings can strengthen small groups. Simple rituals of opening and closing, such as the lighting and extinguishing of a candle or ringing of a small bell, can effectively mark time as sacred, as set apart, and acknowledge its ending as well. The sharing of personal stories, either by themselves or in conjunction with the reading of biblical or other sacred texts, are deepened by careful attending by others whom the storyteller trusts. After absorbing the narrative, questions about missing details of the story or inquiries about what the story meant to its teller can strengthen a sense of shared memories within the group. Imaginative reconstructions of stories can free group members from a sense of "fixedness" about the past. Small groups have a marked advantage in their opportunities to experiment with ritual and story practices.

Small groups can be vulnerable to the same charges of individualism that have faced other contemporary religious practices, particularly when they are built on psychotherapeutic models. By attending to each others' stories and by ritualizing the larger stories of the community, small groups may actually help members deepen their consciousness of, and commitments to, the plight of others beyond themselves. In addition, small groups that remain consistent over time can deepen a sense of shared memories as the group authors its own story.

Prayer and Meditation

Neurological "pictures" of praying brains can be disconcerting. "This is your brain. This is your brain on prayer." It's seldom said in quite those words, but research like that undertaken by neuropsychiatrists Andrew Newberg and Eugene d'Aquili is providing intriguing pictures of the brains of experienced meditators.[9] Describing our most profound experiences of communion with God in terms of the autonomic nervous system and the loss of input to particular areas of the brain would appear to rob prayer of its sacredness and faith of its object. That our expanded senses of space may result from decreased input to the brain's right orientation area (which is responsible for our spatial orientation) borders on sacrilege. Reading that our sense of connection with others may be caused by decreased input to the brain's left orientation area (which is responsible for our awareness of personal boundaries) threatens to turn our experiences of God into a case of misfiring neurons.

Yet discoveries of the brain's responses to spiritual experience and conviction can support as well as deny the reality of our experiences of God. The fact that neuroscientists can picture our brains recognizing a loved one surely does nothing to undermine our conviction of that person's real presence! What such studies do offer us is a demonstration of the essential embodiment of our thinking, feeling, and even our praying. We are built to pray, confirming our experience that prayer comes from deep within us — even from beyond us (Rom. 8:26).

---

9. Eugene d'Aquili and Andrew B. Newberg, *The Mystical Mind: Probing the Biology of Religious Experience* (Minneapolis: Fortress Press, 1999); Andrew Newberg, Eugene d'Aquili, and Vince Rause, *Why God Won't Go Away: Brain Science and the Biology of Belief* (New York: Ballantine, 2001).

Profound prayer may in fact be grounded in our earliest experiences of separation at birth.[10] The infant's first "cry for the other" at the moment of birth is both a cry of separation and a cry for connection.[11] At one and the same time, we experience loss and longing for reunion, a pattern that shapes our experiences and practices of faith throughout life's course. Deep prayer literally emanates from the deepest fibers of our being.

Pictures of the meditating brain also offer scientists ways to speculate about the differences between prayer that uses tangible objects as pathways to experiencing the divine (called kataphatic, or "with image") and prayer that eschews images (known as apophatic, or "without image").[12] When the brain focuses attention on an object in the environment (a cross, a picture of Jesus), visual signals travel to the visual cortex and then through brain areas where the image makes rich associations with other memories, including emotional ones. The arousal system appears to be gradually activated in kataphatic prayer, producing a gentle sense of excitement. Focusing on images in memory involves similar brain structures, though attention is focused on recall rather than on direct sensory input.

In apophatic prayer, the brain intentionally restricts input from sensory stimuli and from left-hemisphere verbal-conceptual locations. The left hemisphere's interpreter is turned off for a while and a profound sense of quiet ensues. Input is thereby also limited to orientation areas in the brain which provide our sense of spatial location and boundaries to the self. As we noted above, these changes in input contribute to a sense of extended space and loss of ego boundaries. In apophatic prayer, the quiescent system is activated, eventually producing deep relaxation. Descriptions of these brain processes are complex, and yet they give further evidence of the distinctive

10. Perry LeFevre, "Prayer," in Hunter, *Dictionary of Pastoral Care and Counseling,* 937–39.

11. James Ashbrook, "The Cry for the Other: The Biocultural Womb of Human Development," *Zygon* 29, no. 3 (September 1994).

12. d'Aquili and Newberg, *The Mystical Mind,* 110–16.

qualities of our experiences of prayer. Neurology demonstrates the groundedness of spiritual life in the very cells of our bodies.

Memory and imagination are active participants in prayer and meditation, though they find different roles to play in the two different approaches to prayer. Image-focused prayer follows quite closely the model we proposed in chapter 1, whether those images are immediately present or remembered. The brain's natural propensity to make associations with objects it is perceiving helps us comprehend the richness images take on during contemplation. Our brains naturally pick an object out of the environment for our attention, allowing other stimuli to recede into the background. In day-to-day living, attention shifts automatically and unconsciously from one object to another. In meditation, in contrast, that attention is held long enough that the brain gradually drops its sense of distinctness and a sense of closeness and merger becomes possible.

Images therefore connect us with stories whether we consciously remember them or not. The rich association areas of the brain trigger both memory and imagination in prayer much as they do in worship, frequently allowing forgotten stories to reemerge as the past is recalled in the present context of God's experienced presence. New associations become possible as past and future stories are relived in the context of the liminal period of meditation where attention, receptivity, and expectancy prime the brain for transformation and healing. Prayer becomes an opportunity for healing as emotional memories are integrated into a larger story of reunion with the Other. New memories are created, and new trajectories of the soul are given birth.

Apophatic, or image-denying, forms of prayer have been understood as the domain of experienced or "advanced" meditators, since they are undertaken without the support of images. While the current volume argues for the centrality of images as the "coin" of mental and religious life, apophatic prayer or meditation employs the suspension or transcending of (particularly visual) images. No less an authority than the twentieth-century contemplative Thomas Merton declares,

The function of image, symbol, poetry, chant, and of ritual (remotely related to sacred dance) is to open up the inner self of the contemplative, to incorporate the senses and the body in the totality of the self-orientation to God that is necessary for worship and for meditation. Simply to neglect the senses and body altogether, and merely to let the imagination go its own way, while attempting to plunge into a deeply abstracted interior prayer, will end in no result even for one who is proficient in meditation.[13]

Brain studies suggest that either road can lead to our experience of the divine. Two equally viable paths to God are open to us: whether we move more deeply into the images that draw us to God or clear our minds of particulars, either path can move us closer to the reality of the God who is beyond all images we construct.

The accumulated wisdom of centuries has taught us a variety of methods for prayer. While prayer may be grounded in our very beings, prayer and meditation still call for discipline and practice. The impulse to pray is innate. Methods of prayer are learned, just as Jesus taught his disciples to pray. Procedural as well as declarative and episodic memories are all transformed in effective prayer. What we are learning of the brain underscores the fact that prayer relies on the same processes that enable us to relate to others — to need, to communicate, and to care. Much as we learn to speak and care through practice, we also grow in our capacities for prayer. In both our own prayer and our study of the practices of prayer, we too naturally implore, "Teach us to pray."

Hardwired or Rewired?

Throughout the course of this volume we've encountered, if briefly, the stories of four human beings. In our introduction, we met Christina Santhouse, the eight-year-old girl who lost the right half of her

13. Thomas Merton, *Contemplative Prayer* (Garden City, N.Y.: Doubleday, 1969), 85.

brain in a surgery to treat Rasmussen's encephalitis. In chapter 2, we encountered the story of H.M., the twenty-seven-year-old man whose surgery for epilepsy destroyed the hippocampus and took away from him the ability to consolidate new memories. And then there was Phineas Gage, the railroad worker who survived an explosion that sent a steel rod through the front of his brain. Finally, in chapter 4 we met Michael, the man whose wife eventually died of cancer, but who, for a time during her illness, lived "as if" she were healed.

Stories put faces on our theories and on our theologies. And others have collected stories of the personal side of the brain's strangely ordered workings, such as Oliver Sacks's *The Man Who Mistook His Wife for a Hat*. Such stories remind us that our brains are much more than an intriguing exercise in puzzle solving. When we talk of our brains, we are speaking of ourselves.

The four persons mentioned above represent one of the central paradoxes of the brain. On the one hand, our brains come with "prepackaged" capacities and needs — the ability to reach and grasp, to create images of the world and play with those images, the ability to learn and remember, the need to ritualize, and perhaps most important, the need and capacity to relate to others and to God. Those life-preserving capacities depend on particular operations of the brain, and when those operations are interrupted, their capacities are also lost. Computer metaphors, as inadequate as they are, are difficult to avoid. "Hardwired" is the language that has come to name this reality.

At the same time, we marvel at the brain's versatility. The younger the brain, the more versatile it is. Christina's young brain has replicated nearly all the right hemisphere functions in the left. We encounter the brain's remarkable capacity to alter the ways it functions, to learn from experience. Our brains also rewire themselves.

Most of our discoveries about the brain are directed toward understanding and finding remedies for neurological disorders rather than focused on deepening our spiritual lives. While cognitive scientists are increasingly utilizing advanced instruments to study the function of normal, living brains, government and corporate initiatives have historically been invested in responding to critical human suffering, to fix brains that are broken. That is the way it should be. But as a result, it has not been theologians or religious practitioners who are asking the basic research questions of the neurosciences — it is scientists, the mentally ill and their families, politicians, pharmaceutical companies, and financial investors. Theologians and religious leaders have historically been relegated instead to "taking the crumbs from beneath the tables" of neurology research being conducted for other purposes.

There are signs that this is changing. Conferences and publications are appearing more regularly that promote dialogue between the neurosciences and religion, such as the ongoing work of the Templeton Foundation, a conference on "Neuroscience and the Person: Scientific Perspectives on Divine Action" sponsored by the Vatican Observatory and the Center for Theology and the Natural Sciences,[14] and Trinity Institute's conference titled "Who Are We?" We are in the early stages of a burgeoning dialogue between the neurosciences and faith.

The brain sciences are becoming the church's new partners in its commitment to the transformation of persons and communities. Daily we are confirming that the brain is built not only for survival, memory, and thought but also for feeling, relating, caring, imagining, and believing. The deepest dimensions of our humanness emerge in our brains. Our understanding of the imago dei underscores the importance of continuing the quest for more knowledge about the brain. The more we learn of the ways we experience God, the more deeply we may come to know Godself. We stand at this point in history and recall the discoveries that have brought us this far. We can only begin to imagine what we have yet to learn.

---

14. Robert John Russell, Nancey Murphy, Theo C. Meyering, and Michael A. Arbib, eds., *Neuroscience and the Person: Scientific Perspectives on Divine Action* (Vatican City State: Vatican Observatory; Berkeley, Calif.: Center for Theology and the Natural Sciences, 1999).

Glossary

Absolute Unitary Being (AUB): term used by biogenetic structuralists to designate a brief state of alternate consciousness which is the ultimate result of meditation or ritual practice, characterized by a sense of the total loss of boundaries separating the self from the cosmos.

Action potential: electrical impulse produced in a neuron when it is stimulated to its threshold of excitation, usually by neurotransmitters released from the terminal buttons of other neurons.

Amygdala: almond-shaped brain structure near the base of the temporal lobe. The amygdala is part of the limbic system and critically involved in learning and in registering and recalling emotions such as fear.

Anterograde amnesia: loss of the ability to record new memories, while memories from the distant past remain essentially intact.

Apophatic prayer: from the Greek for "without image." Form of prayer characterized by the relinquishment of perceived, remembered, or imagined images, texts, or icons.

Arousal system: a term used by biogenetic structuralists to refer roughly to the sympathetic nervous system (see Autonomic nervous system). It is particularly involved in certain types of ritual experience, as well as response to a real or perceived external stimulus.

Association area: section of cortical tissue responsible for connecting information arriving from other brain regions.

Autonomic nervous system (ANS): a discrete system of neurons within the body responsible for internal regulation of the expenditure

197

of energy. It consists of two opposing subsystems: the sympathetic system, which aids in the release of energy and prepares the body for fight-or-flight, and the parasympathetic system, which helps conserve bodily resources by returning the body to rest.

Axon: generally the longest extension of a neuron, the axon extends from the cell body to the terminal buttons which release neurotransmitters for the communication of information to the dendrites or cell bodies of other neurons.

Binding problem: scientific difficulties in describing how the brain gathers discrete dimensions of perceptions and memories into an image of a coherent whole object.

Brain stem: located at the upper end of the spinal cord, the brain stem is critical in basic life support functions like respiration and blood pressure.

Broca's area: region of the left hemisphere involved in speech production.

Cerebellum: meaning "little brain," a structure including cortex and groups of neurons known as nuclei that lies below and behind the neocortex, connected to the brain stem. It is critical to balance and coordination, and also contributes to focusing of attention.

Cognitive imperative: term used by biogenetic structuralists to describe the human brain's universal need to provide explanations for perceived (particularly novel) events in the environment and in the self.

Concrescence: from process theology and Alfred North Whitehead, the continuous process of becoming, or of becoming concrete.

Conscious: pertaining to mental awareness, alertness, and attention. Distinguished from unconscious, or outside of awareness.

Corpus callosum: thick bundle of fibers connecting the left and right hemispheres of the brain. Patients in whom this structure has been surgically severed (e.g., for treatment of severe epilepsy) are known as "split-brain" patients.

Cortex: from the Latin for "bark," the outermost surface of the brain, consisting of four divisions or lobes: frontal, temporal, parietal, and occipital (see the diagram on p. 31).

Deafferentation: decrease or loss of neuronal input to a particular section of the brain; may be caused by either physical or functional changes and appears to be involved in the temporary experience of oneness in meditation and ritual practice.

Declarative memory: general term for facts or images available for conscious recall. Distinguished from procedural memory (see below).

Dendrites: tree-shaped branches on a cell body responsible for the reception of information from the terminal buttons of other neurons.

Encoding: recording of memories for recall.

Engram: lasting neural traces that constitute a particular memory.

Episodic memory: form of declarative memory which involves the recall of events directly experienced. Distinguished from semantic memory and procedural memory.

Flashbulb memories: autobiographical memories during time of high emotional charge, such as during times of national crisis or personal trauma. Subject to the same distortions of detail as memories recorded during non-emotionally charged events, the general thrust of the story appears to maintain greater accuracy for longer periods of time.

Frontal lobe: covering approximately one-half of the upper front of the human neocortex, the frontal lobe is particularly active in planning, empathy, and working memory.

Gyrus: convolution in the neocortical tissue of the brain, separated by sulci (q.v.) or fissures.

Hippocampus: from the Latin for "seahorse," the hippocampus is part of the limbic system particularly involved in the consolidation of episodic memories and memory for spatial locations. Damage to the hippocampus may produce anterograde amnesia (see above).

Hypothalamus: structure located at the base of the brain (beneath the thalamus) involved in managing the autonomic nervous system and behaviors related to survival (fighting, fleeing, feeding, and sex). It is also connected to the pituitary gland, which controls the release of hormones in the body.

Kataphatic prayer: from the Greek for "with image." Form of prayer which utilizes perceived or remembered images.

Limbic system: subcortical group of brain structures particularly involved in emotional and nurturing behaviors. Includes such structures as the hippocampus, amygdala, thalamus, and hypothalamus.

Liminal: from Latin for "threshold," term used by anthropologists to denote the marginal status of participants in rituals and rites of passage. Represents the "in-between" status of persons who have been removed from their usual roles and surroundings and have not yet returned with a new status.

Long-term potentiation (LTP): lasting change in the response of a postsynaptic cell to messages received from specific presynaptic cells (see Synapse). Induced by repetitive firing, and therefore currently considered the neuronal basis of learning and memory.

Meditation: spiritual practice utilized either by individuals or groups in both Eastern and Western religious traditions for experiences of transcendence or encounter with the divine. May be practiced by focusing on an object or image (see kataphatic prayer) or by relinquishing specific images (see apophatic prayer).

Motor strip: region of the neocortex immediately in front of the central sulcus; involved in movement.

Neocortex: another name for cortex (see above), specifically referring to its evolutionarily late development.

Neuron: nerve cell responsible for transmission of electrical impulses.

Neurotransmitters: chemicals responsible for the transmission of electrical impulses from one neuron to another. Dispensed by the "sending" neuron into its synapse with the "receiving" neuron where they may trigger an action potential.

Occipital lobe: region of the neocortex directly at the back of the brain. Location of the primary visual cortex.

Parasympathetic nervous system: the conserving subsystem of the autonomic nervous system. (See Autonomic nervous system.)

Parietal lobe: upper region of the brain between the frontal and occipital lobes. Contributes to capacities such as face recognition, spatial location, and associations between the other lobes.

Percept: sensory registering of an object in the environment. Distinguished from mental imagery, the label for memories of objects stored in the brain. Images are used in the recognition of percepts.

Plasticity: the brain's capacity to change the relative strength of synaptic connections, that is, its ability to change or "rewire."

Post-traumatic stress disorder (PTSD): known as "shell shock" in World War I, PTSD refers to the long-lasting response to a directly experienced or witnessed trauma, usually involving a threat to life or physical integrity. PTSD is characterized by persistent intrusive memories of the event, accompanied by feelings of fear or helplessness, as well as avoidance of stimuli that provoke painful memories.

Prefrontal cortex: foremost area in the frontal lobe.

Priming: type of memory in which the observer is cued either consciously or unconsciously before a particular task, increasing the likelihood of certain types of response.

Procedural memory: memory for learned skills or tasks. Distinguished from declarative memory for events or facts.

Qualia: discrete dimensions of an object being perceived, such as color, texture, outline.

Quiescent system: a term used by biogenetic structuralists to refer approximately to the parasympathetic nervous system (see Autonomic nervous system). It contributes to the peaceful response to certain types of meditation as well as to conservation of the body's energy resources.

Retrograde amnesia: loss of memory of past events.

Semantic memory: memory for concepts and facts. Distinguished from procedural memory.

Somatosensory cortex: brain region which receives input from sensory neurons in the body; located behind the brain's central sulcus.

Spillover: term applied by biogenetic structuralists to the triggering of the arousal (or sympathetic) system following extreme activation of the quiescent (or parasympathetic) system, or vice versa.

Subcortical: below or inside the brain's neocortex. Generally refers to structures in the limbic system and brain stem.

Sulcus: groove or valley in the neocortex of the brain.

Sympathetic nervous system: subsystem of the autonomic nervous system involved in the "fight-or-flight" response to emotional stimuli.

Synapse: narrow gap between the terminal button of a sending (presynaptic) neuron and the dendritic spine or body of a receiving (postsynaptic) neuron. When an action potential reaches the terminal button of the presynaptic neuron, a chemical neurotransmitter is released into the cleft which triggers a similar response in the postsynaptic neuron.

Temporal lobes: lower lobes on either side of the brain, located roughly inside each ear. Contribute to long-term memory, language (left hemisphere), and music (right hemisphere).

Terminal button: small swelling at the end of an axon; releases chemical neurotransmitters into the synapse with the dendrites or cell bodies of other neurons.

Thalamus: relatively large, two-lobed structure in the middle of the brain which serves as a central relay station to the cortex from other parts of the brain. It is particularly involved in transmitting sensory information to appropriate brain regions.

Unconscious: pertaining to images, concepts, feelings, and neuropsychological mechanisms that are not available to conscious awareness.

Wernicke's area: left temporal lobe region involved in word comprehension.

Working memory: short-term memory involved in executing current tasks. Involves both conscious and unconscious memories.

Bibliography

American Psychiatric Association. *Diagnostic and Statistical Manual of Mental Disorders*. 4th ed. Washington, D.C.: American Psychiatric Association, 1994.

Anderson, Herbert, and Robert Cotton Fite. *Becoming Married*. Louisville: Westminster John Knox Press, 1993.

Anderson, Herbert, and Edward Foley. *Mighty Stories, Dangerous Rituals: Weaving Together the Human and the Divine*. Los Angeles: Jossey-Bass, 1998.

Anderson, Herbert, David Hogue, and Marie McCarthy. *Promising Again*. Louisville: Westminster John Knox Press, 1995.

Andresen, Jensine, ed. *Religion in Mind: Cognitive Perspectives on Religious Belief, Ritual, and Experience*. Cambridge: Cambridge University Press, 2001.

Ashbrook, James. "The Cry for the Other: The Biocultural Womb of Human Development," *Zygon* 29, no. 3 (September 1994).

———. *Minding the Soul: Pastoral Counseling as Remembering*. Minneapolis: Fortress Press, 1996.

Ashbrook, James, and Carol Rausch Albright. *The Humanizing Brain: Where Religion and Neuroscience Meet*. Cleveland: Pilgrim Press, 1997.

Bell, Catherine. *Ritual Theory, Ritual Practice*. New York: Oxford University Press, 1992.

Benson, Herbert, with Marg Stark. *Timeless Healing: The Power and Biology of Belief*. New York: Scribner, 1996.

Boyer, Pascal. *Religion Explained*. New York: Basic Books, 2001.

Brown, Warren, Nancey Murphy, and H. Newton Malony, eds. *Whatever Happened to the Soul? Scientific and Theological Portraits of Human Nature*. Minneapolis: Fortress Press, 1998.

Burkhart, John E. *Worship: A Searching Examination of the Liturgical Experience*. Philadelphia: Westminster Press, 1982.

Carlson, Neil R. *Physiology of Behavior*. Boston: Allyn & Bacon, 1977.

Clebsch, William A., and Charles R. Jaekle. *Pastoral Care in Historical Perspective.* New York: Harper Torchbooks, 1967.

Cobb, John, Jr., and David Ray Griffin. *Process Theology: An Introductory Exposition.* Philadelphia: Westminster Press, 1976.

Cull, Peter, ed. *The Sourcebook of Medical Illustration.* New York: Parthenon, 1989.

Damasio, Antonio. *Descartes' Error: Emotion, Reason, and the Human Brain.* New York: G. P. Putnam's Sons, 1994.

———. *The Feeling of What Happens: Body and Emotion in the Making of Consciousness.* New York: Harcourt Brace, 1999.

Damasio, Hannah, Thomas Grabowski, Randall Frank, Albert M. Galaburda, and Antonio R. Damasio. "The Return of Phineas Gage: Clues About the Brain from the Skull of a Famous Patient." *Science,* new series 264, no. 5162 (May 20, 1994): 1102–5.

d'Aquili, Eugene G., Charles D. Laughlin Jr., and John McManus. *The Spectrum of Ritual: A Biogenetic Structural Analysis.* New York: Columbia University Press, 1979.

d'Aquili, Eugene, and Andrew B. Newberg. *The Mystical Mind: Probing the Biology of Religious Experience.* Minneapolis: Fortress Press, 1999.

Deacon, Terrence W. *The Symbolic Species: The Co-Evolution of Language and the Brain.* New York: W. W. Norton, 1997.

de Rivera, Joseph, and Theodore Sarbin. *Believed-In Imaginings: The Narrative Construction of Reality.* Washington, D.C.: American Psychological Association, 1998.

Driver, Tom. *The Magic of Ritual: Our Need for Liberating Rites That Transform Our Lives and Our Communities.* New York: HarperCollins, 1991.

Edelman, Gerald M., and Giulio Tononi. *A Universe of Consciousness: How Matter Becomes Imagination.* New York: Basic Books, 2000.

Fulghum, Robert. *From Beginning to End: The Rituals of Our Lives.* New York: Ivy Books, 1995.

Gardner, Howard. *Frames of Mind: The Theory of Multiple Intelligences.* New York: Basic Books, 1983.

Gazzaniga, Michael. *The Mind's Past.* Berkeley: University of California Press, 1998.

Gennep, Arnold van. *The Rites of Passage.* London and Henley: Routledge and Kegan Paul, 1960.

Gerkin, Charles. *The Living Human Document: Re-Visioning Pastoral Counseling in a Hermeneutical Mode.* Nashville: Abingdon Press, 1984.

Goleman, Daniel. *Emotional Intelligence*. New York: Bantam Books, 1995.

Gould, Elizabeth, Alison J. Reeves, Michael S. A. Graziano, and Charles Gross. "Neurogenesis in the Neocortex of Adult Primates," *Science* 286 (October 15, 1999): 548–52.

Grimes, Ronald L. *Beginnings in Ritual Studies*. Revised edition. Columbia: University of South Carolina Press, 1995.

————. *Deeply into the Bone: Reinventing Rites of Passage*. Berkeley: University of California Press, 2000.

Hogue, David A. "Shelters and Pathways: Ritual and Pastoral Counseling," *Journal of Supervision and Training in Ministry* 19 (1999): 57–67.

Hunter, Rodney J., ed. *Dictionary of Pastoral Care and Counseling*. Nashville: Abingdon Press, 1990.

Imber-Black, Evan, Janine Roberts, and Richard Whiting, eds. *Rituals in Families and Family Therapy*. New York: W. W. Norton, 1988.

Jourdain, Robert. *Music, the Brain, and Ecstasy: How Music Captures Our Imagination*. New York: Avon Books, 1997.

Keshgegian, Flora. *Redeeming Memories: A Theology of Healing and Transformation*. Nashville: Abingdon Press, 2000.

Koenig, Harold G., Michael E. McCullough, and David B. Larson. *Handbook of Religion and Health*. New York: Oxford University Press, 2001.

Kosslyn, Stephen M. *Image and Brain: The Resolution of the Imagery Debate*. Cambridge, Mass.: MIT Press, 1994.

Lartey, Emanuel. *In Living Colour: An Intercultural Approach to Pastoral Care and Counselling*. London: Cassell, 1997.

Laughlin, Charles D., Jr., John McManus, and Eugene G. d'Aquili. *Brain, Symbol and Experience: Toward a Neurophenomenology of Human Consciousness*. New York: Columbia University Press, 1992.

LeDoux, Joseph. *The Emotional Brain: The Mysterious Underpinnings of Emotional Life*. New York: Touchstone, 1996.

————. *Synaptic Self: How Our Brains Become Who We Are*. New York: Viking, 2002.

Lester, Andrew. *Hope in Pastoral Care and Counseling*. Louisville: Westminster John Knox Press, 1995.

MacLean, Paul. *The Triune Brain in Evolution: Role in Paleocerebral Functions*. New York: Plenum Press, 1990.

McAdams, Dan. *Stories We Live By: Personal Myths and the Making of the Self*. New York: William Morrow, 1993.

Merton, Thomas. *Contemplative Prayer.* Garden City, N.Y.: Doubleday, 1969.

Mitchell, Kenneth R., and Herbert Anderson. *All Our Losses, All Our Griefs: Resources for Pastoral Care.* Philadelphia: Westminster Press, 1983.

Morrill, Bruce T. *Anamnesis as Dangerous Memory: Political and Liturgical Theology in Dialogue.* Collegeville, Minn.: Liturgical Press, 2000.

Neuger, Christie. *Counseling Women: A Narrative, Pastoral Approach.* Minneapolis: Fortress Press, 2001.

Newberg, Andrew, Eugene d'Aquili, and Vince Rause. *Why God Won't Go Away: Brain Science and the Biology of Belief.* New York: Ballantine, 2001.

Ornstein, Robert. *The Right Mind.* New York: Harcourt Brace, 1997.

Patton, John. *Pastoral Care in Context: An Introduction to Pastoral Care.* Louisville: Westminster John Knox Press, 1993.

Pinel, John. *Biopsychology.* Boston: Allyn & Bacon, 1990.

Pinker, Steven. *How the Mind Works.* New York: W. W. Norton, 1997.

Preston, Stephanie D., Antoine Bechara, Thomas J. Grabowski, Hannah Damasio, and Antonio R. Damasio. "A Perception-Action Model of Cognitive Empathy? A PET Investigation of Imagining Your Own Experience and Someone Else's." University of Iowa Hospitals and Clinics; Department of Neurology, Iowa City, Iowa, 2002.

Preston, Stephanie D., and Frans B. M. de Waal. "Empathy: Its Ultimate and Proximate Bases." *Behavioral and Brain Sciences* 25 (February 2002): 1–20.

Pribram, Karl H., ed. *On the Biology of Learning.* New York: Harcourt, Brace & World, 1969.

Ramshaw, Elaine. *Ritual and Pastoral Care.* Minneapolis: Fortress Press, 1987.

Rappaport, Roy. *Ritual and Religion in the Making of Humanity.* Cambridge: Cambridge University Press, 1999.

Ratey, John J. *A User's Guide to the Brain: Perception, Attention, and the Four Theaters of the Brain.* New York: First Vintage Books, 2002.

Ruby, Perrine, and Jean Decety. "Effect of Subjective Perspective Taking During Simulation of Action: A PET Investigation of Agency." *Nature Neuroscience* 4, no. 5 (May 2001): 546–50.

Russell, Robert John, Nancey Murphy, Theo C. Meyering, and Michael A. Arbib, eds. *Neuroscience and the Person: Scientific Perspectives on Divine Action.* Vatican City State: Vatican Observatory; Berkeley, Calif.: Center for Theology and the Natural Sciences, 1999.

Sacks, Oliver. *The Man Who Mistook His Wife for a Hat.* New York: Summit Books, 1985.

Schacter, Daniel L., ed. *Memory Distortion: How Minds, Brains, and Societies Reconstruct the Past.* Cambridge, Mass.: Harvard University Press, 1995.

————. *Searching for Memory: The Brain, the Mind, and the Past.* New York: Basic Books, 1996.

————. *The Seven Sins of Memory: How the Mind Forgets and Remembers.* Boston: Houghton Mifflin, 2001.

Shapiro, Francine, and Margot Silk Forrest. *Eye Movement Desensitization and Reprocessing: The Breakthrough Therapy for Overcoming Anxiety, Stress, and Trauma.* New York: Basic Books, 1997.

Stern, Daniel N. *The Interpersonal World of the Infant: A View from Psychoanalysis and Developmental Psychology.* New York: Basic Books, 1985.

Ulanov, Ann and Barry. *The Healing Imagination: The Meeting of Psyche and Soul.* Einsiedeln, Switzerland: Daimon, 1999.

van der Hart, Onno. *Rituals in Psychotherapy: Transition and Continuity.* New York: Irvington Publishers, 1983.

Wimberly, Edward P. *African American Pastoral Care.* Nashville: Abingdon Press, 1991.

Zack, Jeffrey M., Todd S. Braver, Margaret A. Sheridan, David I. Donaldson, Abraham Z. Snyder, John M. Ollinger, Randy L. Buckner, and Marcus E. Raichle. "Human Brain Activity Time-Locked to Perceptual Event Boundaries," *Nature Neuroscience* 4, no. 6 (June 2001).

Index

211